DAN YR OGOF

Dan yr Ogof

THE JEWEL OF WELSH CAVES

MARTYN FARR

First impression—1999

ISBN 1 85902 645 1

© text and illustrations (unless otherwise stated) : Martyn Farr

Printed in Wales by
Gomer Press, Llandysul, Ceredigion

This book is dedicated
to the memory of
Pete Fowler,
my caving companion and friend.

Contents

Acknowledgements

To publish a book of this nature requires the help of many people and organisations: I thank the Ordnance Survey for permission to publish the map extract on page 10, and David Judson for permitting the reproduction of the Dan yr Ogof cave survey. Peter Fowler must take special thanks for preparing the various maps and diagrams.

In the field of historical research, I am particularly indebted to the late Alan Coase for documenting much of the early exploration. The various newsletters and journals of the South Wales Caving Club have also proved invaluable. For the loan of photographs I thank Joan Coase, Dig Hastilow, Carole Morgan Hopkins, David Hunt and Ashford Price. The photographic assistance provided by my long-suffering caving companions, in particular Pete Fowler who never shirked from load-carrying or any other onerous task associated with underground photography, is also gratefully acknowledged. Likewise, for his patience, understanding and constructive criticism relating to the text, I am particularly indebted to my good friend Pat Cronin.

Finally, on behalf of all cavers, a special note of thanks must be extended to the proprietor of Dan yr Ogof showcaves, Ashford Price, for his encouragement and support of all our caving activities throughout the years.

MARTYN FARR

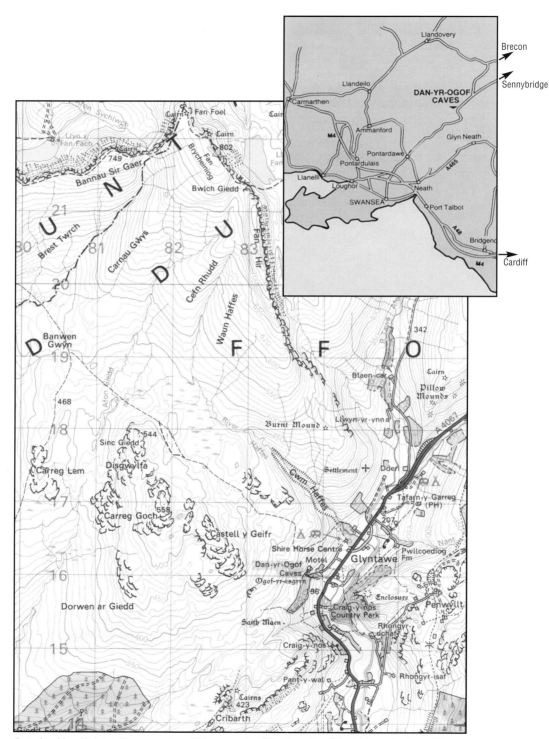

Reproduced from Ordnance Survey mapping with the permission of The Controller of Her Majesty's Stationery Office
© Crown Copyright, licence no. MC 88199M.

Foreword

Caves are to be found in most countries of the world. Those of the British Isles have long been known amongst travellers— places such as Wookey Hole and Cheddar Caves in Somerset, Peak Cavern in Derbyshire and the famous pothole Gaping Gill in Yorkshire. In Wales it is Dan yr Ogof which takes pride of place. This is the foremost showcave complex in the country and arguably the finest of its kind in the British Isles, visited by well over 200,000 people each year. Apart from the other attractions of this magnificent site on the western flank of the upper Swansea valley, here the visitor may wander at leisure through three separate caves: the original Dan yr Ogof, where a mighty torrent is discharged from the Black Mountain; Cathedral Cave, aptly named after the sheer immensity of the tunnel leading back into the mountainside; and, last but not least, Ogof yr Esgyrn (the Bone Cave), originally an important archaeological site but today an interpretive centre transporting the visitor back in time some 2000 years or more.

During the twentieth century some of the longest, deepest and most challenging cave explorations in the British Isles have been undertaken in the upper Swansea valley. This book deals specifically with the exploration of Dan yr Ogof and its hinterland, where a series of outstanding discoveries has led to the establishment of some of Britain's longest cave networks, classic caves of international renown.

The story begins in 1912 when the Morgan brothers, from nearby Abercrave, mounted a series of audacious visits deep into the hillside. Ill-prepared by the standards of modern-day explorers and equipped with only the most basic lighting and other gear, the pair overcame climbs, deep pools and rugged terrain. A quarter of a century later the sport of caving had come of age and some of the leading explorers in Britain quietly set their sights upon the area's evident potential. At Dan yr Ogof, in particular, the prospect of a substantial river cave seemed likely, a major cave system extending far beneath the Black Mountain towards Sinc y Gïedd to the north-west. The ventures of the Dragon Group, as they were known, did not go unrewarded. Their explorations in 1937 more than doubled the known length of the cave and the finds gave a clear indication as to the fabulous nature of the cave that must surely lie ahead.

It was 1966 before these hopes were realised, when an attractive young lady from the village of Crai successfully negotiated the claustrophobic confines of the Long Crawl. Beyond lay scarcely imaginable wonders, huge chambers carved in jet black rock and fabulous arrays of straw stalactites which left the explorers awestruck. Their overwhelming sense of excitement is evident in the names given to new found passageways: Flabbergasm Chasm, Cloud Chamber, and the Abyss. Since the late 1960s explorers have been required to adopt more extreme techniques to further the quest. The determination and danger involved in the activity of cave divers warrant detailed description of their methods for their role will probably be of crucial importance in the future.

Because caves such as Dan yr Ogof have been known for many years, people are often surprised to learn that many

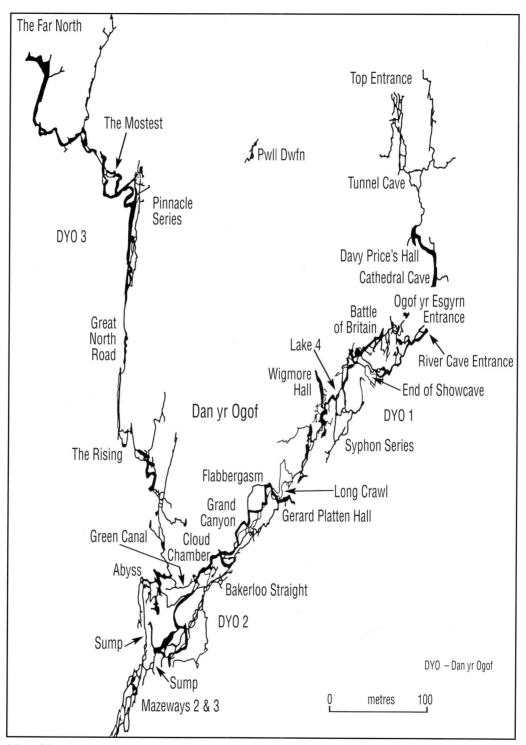

The Far North

The Mostest

Pinnacle
Series

DYO 3

Great
North
Road

The Rising

Dan yr Ogof

Pwll Dwfn

Top Entrance

Tunnel Cave

Davy Price's Hall
Cathedral Cave

Ogof yr Esgyrn
Entrance

Battle
of Britain

River Cave Entrance

Lake 4

Wigmore
Hall

End of Showcave

DYO 1

Syphon Series

Flabbergasm

Long Crawl

Grand
Canyon

Gerard Platten Hall

Green Canal

Cloud
Chamber

Abyss

Bakerloo Straight

DYO 2

Sump

DYO – Dan yr Ogof

Sump

0   metres   100

Mazeways 2 & 3

Map of Dan yr Ogof and Cathedral Cave (from survey by D. M. Judson).

12

miles of tunnels are still unaccounted for. The known passageways have been traced over a distance in excess of 16 km (10 miles), yet cavers believe that the entire complex might well be double or even three times this length. This is a classic story of challenge and exploration—a tale far from complete, for many exciting discoveries await those who are prepared to explore the extremities of the known system. It is known, for example, that the water which disappears into small fissures in the vicinity of Carreg Lem, over two miles west-north-west of the showcave entrance, eventually finds its way to Dan yr Ogof. One day, perhaps many years in the future, cavers may travel this route.

In the search for new routes perseverance and determination are essential qualities. But every explorer also needs a little luck. Removal of a single rock from a partially blocked tunnel or the careful re-examination of some obscure part of a cave may yield a new avenue of approach. The excitement generated when yours is the first light ever to shine in some hitherto unknown section of the underworld is almost indescribable.

As the physical exploration of caves proceeds, we are slowly developing a better understanding of their evolution. Today, a wealth of scientific data and technical knowledge is being massed, which in due course will prove invaluable in unlocking the secrets of this and many other limestone areas of the world. Much remains to be learnt and for all those people who visit caves on a regular basis this is part of the fascination of the pastime.

The aim of this lavishly illustrated book is to convey the excitement of caving in the Dan yr Ogof area, the wonders that have been revealed and the challenge which still confronts explorers today. Dan yr Ogof boasts some of the most beautiful systems in the world and hopefully this account will aid the understanding of caves and caving among members of the public.

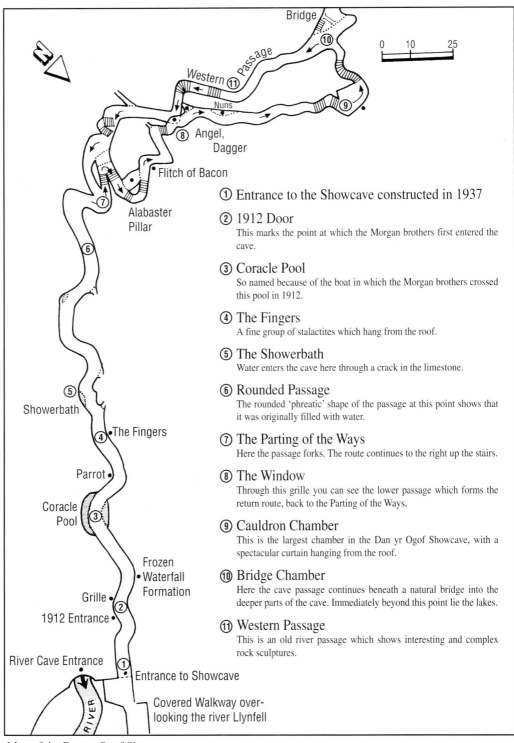

① **Entrance to the Showcave constructed in 1937**

② **1912 Door**
This marks the point at which the Morgan brothers first entered the cave.

③ **Coracle Pool**
So named because of the boat in which the Morgan brothers crossed this pool in 1912.

④ **The Fingers**
A fine group of stalactites which hang from the roof.

⑤ **The Showerbath**
Water enters the cave here through a crack in the limestone.

⑥ **Rounded Passage**
The rounded 'phreatic' shape of the passage at this point shows that it was originally filled with water.

⑦ **The Parting of the Ways**
Here the passage forks. The route continues to the right up the stairs.

⑧ **The Window**
Through this grille you can see the lower passage which forms the return route, back to the Parting of the Ways.

⑨ **Cauldron Chamber**
This is the largest chamber in the Dan yr Ogof Showcave, with a spectacular curtain hanging from the roof.

⑩ **Bridge Chamber**
Here the cave passage continues beneath a natural bridge into the deeper parts of the cave. Immediately beyond this point lie the lakes.

⑪ **Western Passage**
This is an old river passage which shows interesting and complex rock sculptures.

Map of the Dan yr Ogof Showcave

14

Dan yr Ogof – The Jewel of Welsh Caves

Dan yr Ogof is Wales' most well known cave. Arguably it is the finest showcave complex in the British Isles, if not western Europe. What few people appreciate, however, is the true splendour of the underworld hereabouts, not only beyond the limits of public access in Dan yr Ogof but also in the area at large. Deep beneath the Black Mountain and adjoining upland areas lie scarcely imaginable sights. These are some of the world's classic caves.

At the head of the Swansea valley the scenery is rugged and wild. The backdrop is the Carmarthenshire Fans, a stark and desolate range of mountains, on whose southern slopes small streams disappear into the earth over a wide area. Far below the surface these converge to form a substantial river which bursts forth from the ground at Dan yr Ogof. Freed from its rocky confines the river Llynfell is full of youthful vigour, cascading through the wooded ravine to join the Tawe close to the majestic, soaring buttress at Craig-y-nos. The vast outpouring is from a huge cavernous entrance, assuredly a portal to another world; a strange world, hewn from blue-black rock by the powerful hand of nature. It is a realm of permanent darkness;

A family group stop to examine an interesting rock formation in the showcave section of Dan yr Ogof.

few lights ever shine in these subterranean corridors; visitors here are as transient as a falling meteor, a fleeting trace of light, then gone.

The upper Swansea valley is a world apart from the clamour of the populous south. Passing northwards through the rocky defile at Craig-y-nos, industrial South Wales is left far behind. This is a most spectacular gateway to the Brecon Beacons National Park. Mountains rise above the valley floor which lies ahead; to the left the long straight edge of Fan Hir, while the distant skyline to the right is dominated by the dark brooding mass of Fan Gyhirych.

The entrance to Dan yr Ogof river cave in the depths of winter.

The upper Swansea valley, looking north, from Cribarth mountain. Craig-y-nos Castle lies in the foreground, whilst the main road can be seen heading north towards Brecon. Fan Gyhirych is the high summit, on the right, while Dan yr Ogof lies on the western flank of the valley, less than half a mile beyond Craig-y-nos.

Dan yr Ogof and the Black Mountain as seen from Craig y Rhiwarth, on the east side of the Swansea valley.

Their very names evoke an air of mystery. Southwards, the view is dominated by the craggy, hummocky mass known as Cribarth, once connected to the hill on the eastern side of the valley before the river Tawe carved its present course. Today the river sidesteps through this rocky barrier leaving a gorge-like setting at Craig-y-nos, from which the gothic-style castle, once the home of Madame Adelina Patti-Nicoloni (later Baroness Cederstrom), the nineteenth-century international opera star, takes its name. At the base of a thickly wooded gully, less than half a mile north of Craig-y-nos, lies Dan yr Ogof.

That part of the Tawe valley in which Dan yr Ogof is situated is very different in appearance, largely due to changes in the nature of the rock. It is a particular rock type that accounts for, and contributes to the size and beauty of the caves. The caves owe their existence to a band of limestone which encircles the South Wales coalfield, a rock which over a period of many, many tens of thousands of years has been dissolved and eroded very slowly to produce the features encountered today.

Caves such as Dan yr Ogof depend on three things for their existence: soluble rock, a constant flow of water, and time. Limestone, unlike the Old Red Sandstone of the Carmarthenshire Fans, is soluble in mildly acidic water. Due to geological upheavals in the dim distant past the high mountains to the north provide the gathering ground for several streams which flow southwards onto the limestone of the Black Mountain, a rock broken by horizontal (bedding planes) and vertical cracks (joints). It is into these natural fissures that water quietly seeps, under the influence of gravity.

Given access to the heart of the limestone, the water begins its dual function of destruction and construction.

Initially, the water simply dissolves the rock. (This is due to the fact that as rainwater passes through the atmosphere it absorbs carbon dioxide to form a mild carbonic acid capable of dissolving calcium carbonate, the main constituent of limestone.) Later, when one particular crack reaches a critical size, it will capture the water seeping through fissures in the surrounding rock. With increased flow, the process is accelerated and slowly, ever so slowly, a seeping, waterlogged fissure will be transformed to a cave.

In the very earliest or **phreatic** stage of cave development the underground passage will be completely flooded. Later, when water levels drop—which happen when major rivers carve ever deeper into their valley floors, or as glaciers gouge and over-deepen their channels—some passageways will be partially drained, and occupied by a free-flowing stream which cuts down into the cave floor. Other ancient waterways will be completely abandoned and are thereafter referred to as **fossil** passages.

Passages which were once completely full of water have distinctive round or elliptical cross-sections. During the later **vadose** stage of development, however, when a stream flows along the cave floor below an airspace, a cave frequently exhibits a trench-like appearance in contrast to the wonderful tubular shapes of first stage passages. Indeed, second stage passages are frequently in the form of tall, narrow fissures or canyons. Many passages will demonstrate elements of both these features, and in cross section they possess a typical 'key-hole' profile, a circular form above a narrow fissure.

Other features associated with the erosional sculpting of the cave are deep shafts or potholes, and large chambers or caverns. Potholes are found at places where water, at some stage in the past, found an easy vertical route, down through the rock layers. Caverns often form where two major fissures intersect, and their floors are frequently littered with boulders which have collapsed from the roof above.

Changes above ground, such as the climatic change that occurs at the onset of an ice age, will also have an effect upon the underworld. When the surface of the land is blanketed in snow and ice, less water enters the cave and consequently little erosion takes place. Later, when the ice melts, dramatic floods may wash mud and stones into cave entrances, possibly blocking the point at which water originally found its way underground. Later still, the stream may re-excavate the old watercourse or even find a new route underground. The evidence for such changes is visible within the caves to all those who care to stop and look. Indeed, caves are a repository of untold knowledge. Time brings about many changes but the mysterious world beneath our feet can tell us much about the evolution of the land on which we live.

En route to the furthest reaches of Ogof Ffynnon Ddu, cavers must negotiate several sections of passage like this—the Traverses. There are several places similar to this in Dan yr Ogof.

In the Lower Series of Dan yr Ogof 2 water has carved a most impressive circular tunnel, named Bakerloo Straight after the London Underground!

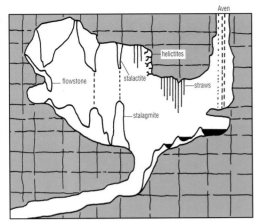

The main cave formations.

Negotiating a fast flowing streamway, a deep lake, a shaft or a claustrophobic crawl is challenging and exciting. But there is more. Although mother nature seeks to carve out and modify passageways through the limestone, so too does she seek to decorate this esoteric world of darkness.

Here and there we find sights of rare, exquisite beauty, in the form of **cave formations**. These decorations are, like the caves themselves, a product of flowing water. As water seeps along fissures in the rock it carries in solution some of the limestone it has dissolved on the way. The acidic water eventually finds its way into an airspace within a cave passage, whereupon it will release some of the dissolved carbon dioxide gas. This, in turn, results in some of the dissolved limestone (calcium carbonate) being precipitated in the form of a white crystalline mineral known as **calcite** (calcium carbonate). A small drop of water emerging on the roof of a cave passage will deposit a minuscule ring of calcite before it falls to the floor. Day after day, year after year, over hundreds or even thousands of years, this process continues and results in the formation of a pure white, delicate **straw stalactite**. Like an ever lengthening

Cloud Chamber, renowned for its delicate arrays of exquisite straw stalactites.

The stalactites and stalagmites in the vicinity of the Skyhook, Ogof Ffynnon Ddu.

calcite-laden waters will produce different but equally spectacular formations—convoluted, ribbed and banded **curtains**. Occasionally, a calcite flow may coat dark cavern walls with a pristine porcelain-like gloss and then meander across the flat cave floor, as is found in the distant cave section known as the Mostest. In the beam of the caver's head-light the sparkling crystals give the appearance of a frozen river. Within such a setting curious little dams and an intricate network of minute ponds are also found, the sides of which are lined with jagged calcite crystals. To cavers these are known as **gour pools**.

The strangest of all cave formations are **helictites**, twisted, branch-like crystalline structures which jut from walls and floors, or even the sides of stalactites. Quite how and why these small, exquisite, gravity-defying features occupy the sites they do is still not properly understood.

Cave formations such as stalactites, stalagmites, pillars, curtains and helictites

drinking straw, or a constantly growing packet of mini Polo mints, the crystalline structure extends downward. Some straw stalactites in Dan yr Ogof are over 2 m in length. Sometimes the hollow at the centre of the straw column will block, causing the water to ooze out just above the constriction. Many years later the stalactite will appear like some pendulous 'carrot-shaped' formation.

When the water droplet falls to the cave floor—provided there is no stream present to wash it away—yet more calcite is laid down. In this case, the accumulating calcite forms a stumpy, solid mass, or **stalagmite**, which grows slowly upward. When a stalactite and stalagmite join, the outcome is a **pillar** or **column**, such as the wonderful formation at the end of Flabbergasm Chasm and the Candlewax formation near Cloud Chamber in Dan yr Ogof. Sometimes the

Pillars above the Skyhook, Ogof Ffynnon Ddu.

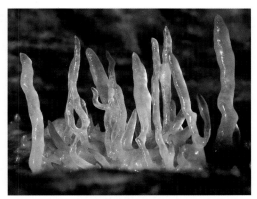
Delicate and almost transparent helictites encrust the walls of the Canyon.

range in size and colour but what is paramount is that they remain as first discovered. A crystal structure which may have taken thousands of years to form can be destroyed in the blink of an eye, a priceless wonder lost for all time.

*   *   *

Man's association with caves has a long and fascinating history and nowhere more so than in the Swansea valley. The very naming of the place is curious for Dan yr Ogof means 'below the cave'! For those first early settlers in the area, the cold, wet, flood-prone river cave held little attraction; they would have been far more interested in a small, discreet hole set in the side of the craggy ravine high above. Ogof yr Esgyrn (the Bone Cave), situated some 40 m above the cavernous mouth of the river cave, was in early times referred to simply as Yr Ogof (The Cave). It was here that human bones were found at an early date, clearly bearing witness to death or burial some time in the dim and distant past. But who would want to scale these precipitous rocky slopes and why? For answers to such questions we must seek the help of archaeologists.

In days gone by archaeology had a reputation for being a somewhat dry and crusty subject, of interest only to academics. Today, however, interest in the subject has been fired by imaginative site interpretation, as is the case in Ogof yr Esgyrn which recalls some of the truly fascinating discoveries made in the caves of the upper Swansea valley.

A number of caves in South Wales have shed invaluable light upon man's history. Excavations in places such as Paviland Cave on the south coast of the Gower peninsula have revealed a wealth of material dating back to the upper Palaeolithic period—the Old Stone Age—indicative of human settlement in the area possibly as early as 36,000 BC. Indeed, this is one of the richest upper Palaeolithic sites in the British Isles.

A family group silhouetted in the entrance of the impressive Bacon Hole, on the Gower peninsula. Archaeological finds in this spacious cave included bones of straight-tusked elephant, slender-nosed rhinoceros, bison, red deer, hyena and cave bear. An early Iron Age bowl was also discovered within the cave.

Most cave sites excavated to date show that they were no more than natural shelters, which might have been utilised by nomadic hunter-gatherer groups as and when the need arose. Paviland Cave, however, might have been the site of a more permanent camp for it is one of the few places where a human burial has been discovered. The famous 'Red Lady' skeleton (now known to be that of a male, aged around 25 years) dates from about 26,000 years ago and was found in association with animal bones including a mammoth's skull complete with tusks. Sometime later the cave would probably have been abandoned altogether because 20,000 years ago Wales was in the grip of an Ice Age, the greater part of the land surface being buried beneath an ice sheet. As climatic conditions slowly improved after the close of the last Ice Age, some 10,000 years ago, the region would have been gradually reoccupied by both man and beast.

By the early Bronze Age, about 3,000-4,000 years ago, there is certainly evidence to suggest that some caves, such as Ogof yr Esgyrn at Dan yr Ogof, were used as more permanent homes. Ogof yr Esgyrn consists of a single chamber about 18 m wide and 11 m long, which today may be entered via a small opening. Situated high on the crags, free of the chilling draught present in the river cave below, people lived here some 3,000 years ago. Generally speaking, we associate Bronze Age people with the great stone circles of Stonehenge and Avebury and circular burial mounds, so common on Salisbury Plain. But here in the Swansea valley their monuments are in the form of standing stones such as Saith Maen, an impressive group of large stones on Cribarth mountain.

On arrival in Wales, these early settlers brought with them a knowledge of metal working. Although the occupation of Ogof yr Esgyrn by Bronze Age dwellers was limited, both in numbers and duration, the archaeological discoveries have proved interesting: a gold bead, the only gold artefact found in the cave; a bronze 'razor' and the blade of a bronze dirk or short sword. This item, 34.3 cm (13.5 inches)

long, is presumed to date between 1050 BC and 850 BC. In all probability occupation of sites such as this would not have been continuous; well hidden, its greatest importance would have been as a point of refuge at times of unrest.

The early Celtic people, of the Iron Age, were the next to settle in the region, about 450 BC. Here in South Wales these people, often referred to as 'Ancient Britons', belonged to a tribe known as the Silures. Evidence has again been found of people living in the cave in the early and late Roman period (sometime between the death of Christ and 400 AD). Indeed, not only did people live here but they also buried their dead in the cave. It is for this reason that the cave was named Ogof yr Esgyrn, the Bone Cave, and probably from this time on the place would have acquired a certain mystique.

A group of the Mendip Exploration Society outside the entrance to the Bone Cave, during the archaeological investigations of the late 1930s.

Photo by Llew Morgan, courtesy of Carole Morgan Hopkins.

The earliest official study of the contents of Ogof yr Esgyrn commenced in 1923, under the guidance of the emminent archaeologist, Sir Mortimer Wheeler, although a more systematic examination of the site was undertaken by Edward Mason in 1938. Reaching the entrance was difficult enough, but the work inside was even more challenging. In its original state the entrance was only half a metre in height and the floor of the chamber beyond the opening was strewn with boulders, partly cemented together by calcite. On one occasion a series of small explosive charges had to be used to blast away a large rock. A surprise lay in store, for underneath the boulder were two Roman coins, together with the remains of a small bag in which they had been kept. In a corner of the chamber lay an area of deep sand and it was here that many human bones were recovered. By the time the study was complete the remains of some forty people had been exhumed. Also found were pieces of pottery, bone pins, bronze awls and a total of nine coins—all providing valuable dating material for the period of occupation.

Excavations such as those conducted in Ogof yr Esgyrn can also be interesting in other ways. It is often stated, for example, that stalactites take thousands of years to form. However, the rate of calcite formation can vary considerably: at Ogof yr Esgyrn, Romano-British pottery was recovered from beneath an 8 cm (3 inch) cover of flowstone, giving an average growth rate of approximately 1 cm every 240 years.

Today, the archaeological study of Ogof yr Esgyrn is complete. The cave has been thoroughly excavated and all bones and human artefacts have been removed. The cave now forms part of the showcave complex and serves as an interpretive centre adorned with a period tableaux and other material illustrating prehistoric life at the site. The life portrayed was fraught with hardship and danger. Apart from tribal quarrels, our ancestors had to contend with wild animals who also sought the shelter of caves in order to raise their young.

Life-size models of some of the animals that probably visited caves are exhibited, including the enormous cave bear, standing over 2.5 m tall when upright, and the smilodon, a savage sabre-toothed member of the cat family. A model of a mammoth can be seen to the rear of the museum and shop.

Bones from Ogof yr Esgyrn set out for viewing on the tables at the Gwyn Arms. This local hostelry was the cavers' base for exploratory operations for many years.
Photo by Llew Morgan, courtesy of Carole Morgan Hopkins.

The Birth of Caving in South Wales

Cave exploration is a slow process: nowhere has this been more evident than at Dan yr Ogof. The major discoveries here have come in short, sharp bursts, spread over a period of almost 100 years. Perhaps our distant ancestors ventured into the entrance in prehistoric times; what is certain, however, is that tallow candles would have provided poor illumination thereby preventing them from venturing far. The main river cave is not only dark, its floor in places is occupied by deep pools and a chilly draught blows through the passageways, posing insurmountable problems for would-be candle-carrying explorers.

One of the first references to the cave appears in the county chronicle compiled by Theophilus Jones in 1805. The entry in *History of Brecknockshire*, today part of the county of Powys, is worthy of note:

On the north of the Tawe a little below the fall of the Tawyne is a rock called Daren yr Ogof, or the rock of the cave. From this springs up at once a sufficient quantity of water for turning a grist mill at all seasons of the year. This brook, or rather a river, called Llynfell (from Llyn a liquid and ell a common termination) ...soon falls into the Tawe; the inhabitants observe that on a rainy day this river does not perceptibly increase, but that on the following day it becomes muddy, and the quantity of water is considerably greater. There is nothing singular in this; the rain falling on the mountain has not only a very considerable depth, but many varieties of soil to penetrate, before it reaches the hollow of this cavern, and consequently a long portion of time is required before the additional water can swell the common current, which is certainly extraordinary . . .

Dan yr Ogof in flood. Under these conditions access to the cave is impossible.

However, if the Dan yr Ogof river cave had been explored for any distance at this time, we have no record of the venture.

Caving in the Swansea valley has been inextricably linked with the development of the sport in Britain in general. For many hundreds of years travellers through Wales had been attracted to the great cavernous entrance to Porth yr Ogof (better known as the White Horse Caves), at the head of the Neath valley. Many awe-inspiring accounts of underground explorations were published by visitors who toured the 'vasty chambers wreathed in cloudy vapours' by the light of candles or flaring torches. Such explorations were driven by curiosity and relatively few dared to venture beyond the daylight zone.

The real spur to the sport of caving in Britain, however, came in the person of a Frenchman, Edouard Albert Martel, who in the summer of 1895 made a brief tour of several limestone regions in the British Isles. It was Martel who made the first successful descent of Gaping Gill, that great chasm in the Yorkshire Dales, and in so doing captured the public imagination and the interest of academic institutions. Prior to this event there had been only occasional forays into the underworld, often prompted by economic motives and by the lure of lead, especially in the case of the Derbyshire Peak District. Few caves were entered purely for sporting reasons until the late nineteenth and early twentieth century.

Prior to this period, cave explorations were few in number and far between. Worthy of mention, however, is the highly significant exploration which took place some 10 miles west of the Swansea valley in the early 1840s. The cave in question is called Llygad Llwchwr (the Eye of the Loughor), a powerful spring, at the foot of the northern slopes of the Black Mountain, about one mile due south of Carreg Cennen castle. One of the earliest references to the cave appears in a letter written in 1698 by Edward Llwyd, the famous Welsh naturalist, although it was the presence of fossils in the limestone, rather than the cave itself, which captured Llwyd's attention:

I have gather'd the Cuthbert Beads or *Entrochi* [i.e. segments of sea lily or crinoid stems], which are the vertebrae of sea starrs, from ye roof of a cave calld Lhygad lhwchwr near Kerrig Kennen Castle . . .

It was here in 1841, about 150 years after Llwyd's visit, that a certain Thomas Jenkins, a cabinet maker of Llandeilo, made the first remarkable underground discoveries in Wales. Although it is no easy 'walk-in' cave, it is clear that Jenkins, with the aid of a rope-ladder and a small collapsible boat, examined most of the underground passageways. An extract from his diary, dated 10 September 1843, follows overleaf:

Llygad Llwchwr is a little known cave at the western extremity of the Black Mountain.

Went together with B. Morgan, David Lewis, John Thomas, Walter Jones, Puddy Combe and Owen Jones to Llygad Llwchwr. Entered the cave at 8.30 a.m. and after turning to the left at right angles to the main branch and getting down over the rock by rope ladder over the stream, we made up the coracle [an oval-shaped craft used by fishermen on the rivers of west Wales] and proceeded down the stream, over very deep pools through several magnificent caverns where man had never dared to before. Came out to daylight at 1.30 p.m.

Over the course of several visits, Jenkins succeeded in reaching the furthest limits of the cave which could be explored without recourse to diving underwater. A sketch plan was prepared, the water temperature was measured at 49°F and the total discharge estimated at 45 hogsheads! Thomas Jenkins also explored in the Ammanford area. Indeed, from his diary entries one gains the impression that he was quite an adventurer.

An account published in *The Handbook of Cardiff and District* (1881) by Ivor James is also intriguing:

Four miles above Craig y Nos, in the Swansea Vale, a cavern, one of three existing there, is, or was, until recently, adorned . . . with beautiful spectacles of stalactite, incrustations which are characteristic of Cheddar. From the central of these caves the headwaters of the river Tawe emerges.

This short entry may not impart a wealth of information regarding early explorations but it certainly illustrates the fact that many knew of the existence of the caves. Ivor James certainly knew of Dan yr Ogof river cave, Ogof yr Esgyrn, and was probably familiar with the stooping-sized tunnel which provided the original access into the showcave, today called Cathedral Cave. One cannot help but wonder whether Ivor James was one of the first to access the initial section of what is today the Dan yr Ogof showcave.

The first acclaimed venture into the Welsh underworld took place in 1912. It was in June of that year when the now famed Morgan brothers entered Dan yr Ogof, thereby ensuring their place in the annals of caving history in the upper Swansea valley. At the time Ashwell and Jeff Morgan were in their thirties and came from a well-to-do local family living at Tŷ Mawr on the outskirts of Abercrave. Their father was the owner of a local colliery, so

Two of the Morgan brothers pose beside the Coracle Pool, close to the entrance of the showcave. This barrier was to be the limit of the first day's exploration in the cave.
Photograph by T. Ashwell Morgan, Ashford Price Collection.

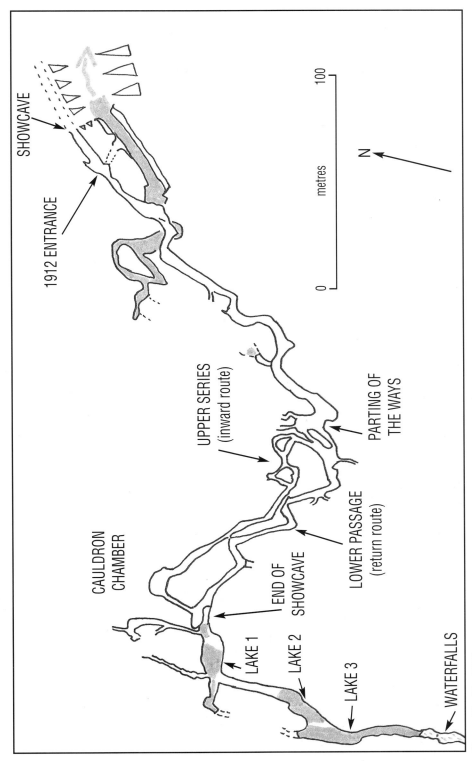

SHOWCAVE

1912 ENTRANCE

CAULDRON CHAMBER

UPPER SERIES (inward route)

PARTING OF THE WAYS

END OF SHOWCAVE

LOWER PASSAGE (return route)

LAKE 1

LAKE 2

LAKE 3

WATERFALLS

N

metres

0   100

Dan yr Ogof in 1912.

27

it is perhaps not surprising that the darkness and confinement below ground posed no fear to his sons. Their experience in the coalmine certainly provided a sound basis for cave exploration. Whether it was straightforward curiosity, or perhaps the lure of possible mineral wealth that led the two young men to the cave on that summer's day in 1912 is not clear, but the brothers were there by choice. Equipped with candles, they carefully examined each wall of the cave until Jeff discovered an opening on the right-hand side just large enough to squeeze through. It was an excited voice that reached Ashwell's ears, for Jeff was standing in a large tunnel of well sculpted rock, adorned here and there with stalactites. Ashwell quickly joined Jeff and the pair then continued along the tunnel for a short distance until their way forward came to an abrupt halt at the edge of a deep pool. Illuminated only by the faint glimmer of candles, it was impossible to tell how far the watery barrier extended. Further progress was impossible without the aid of a boat or raft and as they made their way out of the cave, plans were being made.

The next day Jeff and Ashwell were joined by their brother, Edwin, and Morgan Richard Williams, their gamekeeper. A small raft enabled them to cross the pool of still water which was no more than a few metres long. The four then continued into the darkness along a route that had only ever been traversed by an otter, judging by the footprints in the smooth sand beneath their feet. Several hundred metres into the hillside, they stopped at a point where the passageway split, offering a choice of several different routes.

On the following day they made their third visit, helped on this occasion by their other gamekeeper, William Lewis. On this visit their candles were supplemented by night-lights, which provided better illumination,

and were less likely to be extinguished by draughts or drips from the cave roof. There was a feeling of real adventure in the air for they had taken with them a glass bottle which contained the names of those in the party written on a sheet of paper. The bottle, together with an old thermos flask, was deposited on a ledge close to a 2 m high column of calcite—the Alabaster Pillar. The remains of these two items could be seen in the cave up until the mid 1970s.

On their third and subsequent visits the brothers continued the exploration of the various passageways well beyond formations that were eventually to be named Flitch of Bacon, the Angel, the Dagger, Pillar of Salt and the Three Nuns.

The Three Nuns as they would have appeared to the Morgan brothers in 1912. Owing to the risk of damage, many formations in the showcave are today protected behind a metal grille.

Photo by Llew Morgan, courtesy of Carole Morgan Hopkins.

Eventually they entered a most impressive chamber containing a massive calcite curtain draped from the roof. In the silent world to which they had become accustomed their senses would rapidly have been drawn to a suppressed droning sound that emanated from somewhere not too far ahead. After descending a boulder-strewn slope, a damp mud and sand flood-borne deposit heralded their return to a more 'active' part of the cave. From a ledge or terrace upon which they soon found themselves standing, could be seen a pool of ominously dark water, stretching away into the dim and low-roofed distance. Here the background noise had intensified to an incessant dull roar of what sounded like a fairly substantial waterfall. If they were to continue, then once again a boat would be necessary, only this time it would have to be carried along a fairly demanding route before it could be set upon the dark waters of the underground river.

On their return journey they discovered an alternative route to the Parting of the Ways, the junction close to the Alabaster Pillar. This was doubly fortuitous, for not only was the route slightly shorter but it also removed the need to negotiate several climbs.

After further discussions it was decided to obtain a coracle from Carmarthen. Coracles were traditionally used by fishermen on the relatively placid waters of rivers such as the Tywi and Teifi in west Wales and, viewed at water's edge, such craft might seem altogether ill-suited for any journey over deep water. Most coracles were 1.5 m in diameter and constructed of willow shoots, or any pliable wood suitable for basketmaking, covered by skin or canvas. The final waterproofing was supplied by covering the skin or canvas with pitch. Despite its size and oval shape, the vessel was light and capable of being carried for short distances by one man. In experienced hands they were also highly manoeuvrable.

The next phase of the exploration was about to commence, although on his own admission, Jeffrey Morgan was apprehensive about venturing across a subterranean lake in a coracle:

> Placed on the lake it appeared a frail craft to be entrusted with the mission of carrying a human being into the Stygian darkness into which the lake disappeared.

The distant roaring sound was ominous and strange in more ways than one. It also begged several questions: Was the sound generated by a waterfall plunging into the lake? Or was it a waterfall caused by surplus water leaving the lake? If it proved to be the latter, might the coracle be washed over the brink of the fall and be swept away down some dark tunnel, or would it be swamped? Would it be sucked down by a whirlpool, or be carried away by the stream through low passages? What would happen if an unexpected heavy fall of rain on the surface caused the underground stream to rise?

The walls were black and dark shadows enveloped them. Their breath quietly steamed in front of their faces before drifting away in the cold draught. They were far from the light of day and about to embark upon a great adventure. At a point now known as the Bridge—at the end of the showcave—the small boat was carefully prepared. Cautiously and with some trepidation Ashwell Morgan ventured into the unknown. With a rope attached to the craft, let out by his younger brother Jeff, the pair felt they were in reasonable control of the situation. Lake 1, as it has since become known, was small but even so it was several times the length of the Coracle Pool, the lake which had terminated that first day's exploration. Reaching a low, sloping bank of black rock, Ashwell was able to step out of his craft and report a more impressive railway-sized tunnel heading into the darkness. Jeff soon joined him. However, after having walked but a few metres along the sand-floored passage, the two realised that the coracle would be needed yet again. The craft was quickly brought forward and once more Ashwell took his seat. The rounded coracle was not the easiest craft to manoeuvre and utmost care had to be exercised to avoid colliding with any jagged rocks protruding from either the walls or the lake floor. Slowly the frail craft glided forward, inching its way towards the ever intensifying thunderous roar.

Lake 2 proved to be a 30 m crossing. On its far shore, by a small beach, lay a tiny patch of relatively bright sand beyond which stretched deepening water to both left and right. Once more Jeff was brought forward. The moment of truth was most certainly at hand. As the pair scrutinised the tunnel before them it was evident that the lake that now confronted them was the most daunting so far. The tunnel was more oppressive than a cold, dank dungeon. Scuds of discoloured foam floated ominously past and all the while that terrible noise rumbled somewhere close by. The stout-hearted explorers were now seriously intimidated by their predicament; far from the comfort of a summer's day, their world was dark, damp, chilling and isolated, sapping their energy and insidiously undermining their determination to advance.

Ashwell set out yet again. Easing his way against the flow he soon reached a narrowing and low-roofed section where the tunnel curved away to the left. He was now out of sight, combating an altogether stronger flow racing towards him. With his lamp set inside the craft he could see but a short distance in front of him. Paddling deftly, and straining like some eager young dog on a leash, Ashwell sought to overcome both the current and the rope trailing behind. A couple of minutes later he 'reached a mighty waterfall' whose awe-inspiring roar in that confined space was almost overpowering. There were no small beaches on which to land his frail craft, only narrow ledges jutting from the cave walls, protrusions vaguely reminiscent of old tree roots undermined by the erosive power of a river. With stomach churning, Ashwell gave the signal to return and was steadily pulled back to safety. The two brothers had achieved all that was reasonably possible.

The 1912 explorations were audacious. Prompted in all probability by nothing more than curiosity, they had taken Dan yr Ogof to a length approaching 1 km (half a mile). Unbeknown to the explorers they had established the longest cave in Wales; indeed, it was now one of the longest and most challenging systems in Britain.

For the next twenty-five years Dan yr Ogof received little attention. Caving in Wales was not a pastime undertaken on any regular basis. Indeed, the activity was so sporadic that relatively little was known or published of the explorations that had been conducted in the British Isles as a whole. Caving as a sporting activity commenced in the Yorkshire Dales and in the Mendip Hills of Somerset. Clubs of like-minded individuals were established in these areas and slowly the numbers of participants, and their geographical distribution, began to spread. Interest in the caves of Wales was stimulated by the adventures of the Wessex Cave Club whose members began caving around Pontneddfechan (at the head of the Neath valley) in the years prior to the

Second World War, at a time when there was precious little background information on the geography and geology of limestone areas and no guide books available either for would-be cavers or the growing fraternity of mountaineers and walkers.

September 1936 heralded a new phase of cave exploration in the upper Swansea valley for it was during that month that a noted Yorkshire potholer, Ernest Roberts, visited the area for the first time on a walking holiday. Roberts quickly appreciated the area's potential:

I did the Vans, came down to Sinc y Gïedd, a choked swallet against a little cliff . . . traversed three miles of fell . . . and so down . . . to Dan yr Ogof rising. A cave indeed! I could not cross the flooded beck into the great black entrance, but that did not matter, for at the Gwyn Arms I learnt that the owner and his brothers had been in three quarters of a mile and used a boat.

Later he met Jeffrey Morgan and after

The Lakes in Dan yr Ogof were originally passed using boats. This is a view of Lake 4, first crossed in 1937.

learning how the 1912 exploration had concluded Roberts contacted some of his fellow enthusiasts for he was convinced that, 'A real caving expedition was worthwhile.' One of these early pioneers was Gerard Platten of the Mendip Exploration Society, who together with Roberts was to play a very important role in future expeditions. A visit was planned for the summer of 1937.

pounds and described as a '. . . cross between a baby's bath and a balloon tyre' was their final choice. By today's standards such a craft might appear flimsy or poor but in 1937 this was 'state of the art' equipment; it was certainly better suited to the rigours of the subterranean world than the coracle, illuminated by candles and night-lights, used by the Morgan brothers in 1912.

Events did not turn out as hoped. 'The weather fights for the big caves,' commented Roberts. Dan yr Ogof was hopelessly flooded. A couple of days were to pass before Roberts could record their first undertaking at some length. Having reached what is now the end of the show-cave, the river was clearly audible some way ahead:

Members of the Dragon Group of 1937, outside the Gwyn Arms. Third along the back row is Arthur Hill and next to him is Ted Mason. Crouching in front of them is Don Lumbard, and sitting in front of him (with cigarette) is Gerard Platten.

In May 1937 the team gathered in the valley with a view to exploring Dan yr Ogof which, on the basis of the size of its entrance, the volume of water discharged and the sheer extent of the Black Mountain, could be part of one of the largest cave systems in the British Isles. They had come prepared with an array of caving hardware, including rope-ladders, acetylene carbide lamps and rubber boats. A boat was essential and given the difficulties of transporting any craft underground, an inflatable was the obvious answer. A tiny Franklin Pneumatic Boat, weighing seven

The First Pool [Lake 1] was deep and 12 yards [11m] long but Nelstrop showed us the way; somewhere ahead was a great roar of water. Over a steep bank was a shallower pool, some 20 yards [18m] long, and then we stood on a narrow beach and looked at the Third Pool . . . it simply ran away into darkness. I confess that till we found the Three Pools it had never occurred to me that we were going to be up against pools of the Marble Arch type [a major showcave in Co. Fermanagh, Northern Ireland]. I had thought only of passages of ordinary width and short pools. With that ominous roar ahead we agreed that the Morgans' crossing of 1912 was a great effort.

Their inflatable boat was made ready at Lake 1 and two members of the party made separate attempts to pass the third lake:

On the third pool, Gowing, with string attached, went out over ninety feet [27m] and reported a closing in with a low tunnel discharging a strong current but running askew. He had to cut the string to get back. Nelstrop then went out 140 feet [43 m], got into the tunnel and saw the fall, but with the makeshift paddle the current was far too strong.

Owing to the high water conditions the team had failed to get as far as Ashwell Morgan 25 years previously.

The expedition of May 1937 had been very disappointing with respect to progress in the cave but it did give the team an opportunity to assess the lie of the land and, every bit as important, cement good relations with the Morgan family. Ernest Roberts warmly recalls that,

During the summer Mr T. A. Morgan's old enthusiasm blazed out. Using a two-man boat of wood and canvas with side air chambers, he and Miss Coote and Mr Ashford Price crossed the Coracle Pool [Lake 3] . . . Climbing the side of the low cataract they went 50 yards [46 m] through deep water, and climbing another cataract came under a lower roof to a Fourth Pool stretching into the distance.

A party of cavers exit from the upper side of Lake 3 and head into the cave.

In September (19th & 20th) Ernest Roberts returned to Dan yr Ogof with his friend Gerard Platten, who was accompanied by an 'army' of cavers from Somerset and a new boat, *Red Cymru*. The hospitality which greeted the group is certainly worthy of recall:

Only two southerners were at the supper to which Mr J. L. Morgan entertained us, but a carload arrived at ten, proudly sounding the praises of South Welshmen. From Bristol over Aust Ferry they had worked their way in the dark through the colliery districts, men riding on the step to show them the turns, and good fellows going miles out of their way to pilot them. Three men arrived in the night.

Once more the weather was determined to do its worst and water levels were high. Using their own boat, Ashford Price and Miss Coote, pulling on the roof and sides of the tunnel, made a determined attempt to combat the strong current in Lake 3. All might have been well had not a piece of rock come off the roof and landed in the boat! Their enthusiasm was severely curtailed and they retreated.

Next morning the team were up early and as Roberts records:

Fifteen went in at eight, Baker and I at ten through a dense flash-powder fog. *Cymru* was found soft and could not be blown up, so I arrived at the beach to learn to my joy that nine, including Dr Baker, were over, and the pool definitely lower. Weaver and Harris were first over against an awkward current in the tunnel; Weaver went on ferrying while Wigmore and Harris took *Red Cymru* up the cataracts. Harris found the Fourth Pool, a backwater without visible inlet, but Miss Coote noticed an opening just where one

emerged from under the low roof. Here was an excellent landing and the ferry only 15 yards [14 m].

What followed was to prove an exciting and momentous advance. Within the space of a few metres a short climb gave access to a maze of passageways on several levels. They soon realised, however, that they had parted company with the active river as nearly all the tunnels they explored were silent and dry, a situation very similar to that experienced by the Morgan brothers in 1912.

By the time we returned to the ferries [recorded Roberts], only one acetylene lamp worked feebly; our retreat was made with candles and feeble electric lamps. The water had fallen yet more and one paddled out into the ocean of the Coracle Pool [Lake 3] with the barring spike of Saturday high overhead. Meeting the ferryman and his glimmer reminded one of ships at sea.

In all, ten cavers crossed the lakes that day and came back reporting marvels. The finds included a chamber with fine straw stalactites over 2 m in length (which, in honour of their hosts, they named Ashwell Morgan's Palace), a huge boulder-strewn chamber and numerous side passages. Their discovery was subsequently named the 1937 Series, a section of cave which, combined with that explored in 1912, more than doubled the known length of Dan yr Ogof. Beyond Lake 4 the main river was seemingly lost for the time being.

The increased interest displayed by various English clubs led to Gerard Platten (of the Mendip Exploration Society) founding the Dragon Group, who used the Gwyn Arms, the public house adjacent to Dan yr Ogof, as a base for caving

Within a few metres of leaving the stream at Lake 4, cavers encounter superb formations in the 1937 Series.

Negotiating a small waterfall between Lake 3 and 4.

At the far end of the 1937 Series the passages close down to crawls. The grovel through the Horsetrough marks the start of the Long Crawl.

operations. Several more visits were made to the newly discovered section of cave before the close of 1937. On one such visit Don Lumbard was to comment prophetically:

At last the end of the cave is reached . . . Platten and one or two others had been as far as seemed possible up a particularly filthy way called the Mud Crawl—and quite justifiably, for it is a place where one must crawl with chest in mud about eight inches [20 cm] deep. After many twists and turns around where there was a strong current of air, the way was blocked by what seemed an impossible squeeze at the top of an opening some 5 feet [1.5 m] high. One person, however, did get through, and so another 60 yards [55 m] were added. It still went on but was like a drainpipe half full of water and here it was thought that the river could be heard.

The activities undertaken in 1937 had certainly been challenging and rewarding. In a short space of time the recorded length of the cave increased dramatically from 1 km to well over 2 km (1.5 miles). The setting, sheer size and grandeur of the discoveries, all conspired to raise the awareness of this magnificent cave amongst a wider group of people. Details were recorded in the caving journals and tales of the discoveries also impressed the general public.

The Morgan family had managed to purchase the land surrounding the cave, for there is little doubt that the brothers were fully aware of the site's financial possibilities. They realised that if they could provide easy, dry access to the cave, via a route which avoided the flood-prone river cave, then they were in possession of a potential showcave every bit as good as that at Cheddar or Wookey Hole in Somerset.

Corbel's Chamber, in the 1937 Series.

Given the family's knowledge of mining, there is no doubt that thoughts of opening the first Welsh underground attraction had been maturing for some years.

Dan yr Ogof was a prime objective for cavers visiting South Wales during the late 1930s but, as more interest was generated, other places also came under close scrutiny. In 1937, for example, the Wessex Cave Club made their first descent of the gaping pothole, Pant Mawr Pot, on the mountain east of the Swansea valley. Here a 15 m deep shaft led to a very large passage and streamway. Platten, Roberts and others also explored a short cave in the quarries at Penwyllt (Cwm Dŵr Quarry Caves) overlooking the Swansea valley. The significance of this complex would not be fully appreciated for another 30 years, when some of the most spectacular discoveries ever made established the site (Ogof Ffynnon Ddu) as the longest and deepest cave in the British Isles. Other interesting finds were made in 1938, including the discovery of the remote Pwll Swnd in the heart of the Black Mountain, several miles

The entrance shaft of Pant Mawr.

west of Dan yr Ogof. The caves of the Gower peninsula also came under close scrutiny and Ogof yr Esgyrn, above Dan yr Ogof, was to become a site of major archaeological study.

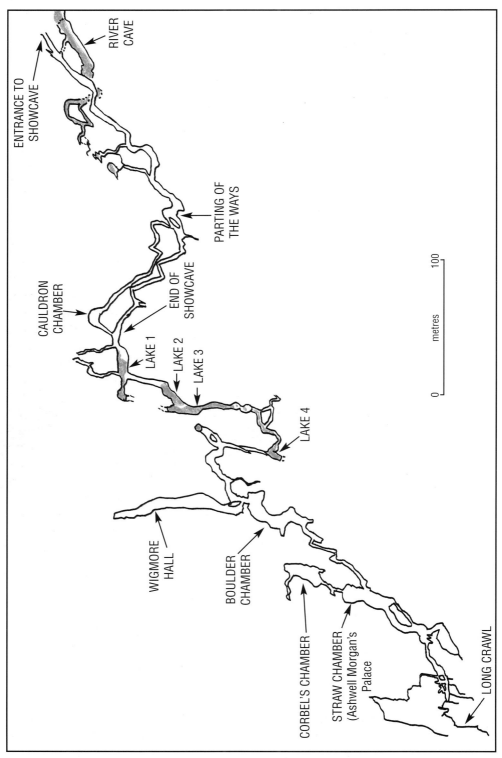

RIVER CAVE

ENTRANCE TO SHOWCAVE

PARTING OF THE WAYS

CAULDRON CHAMBER

END OF SHOWCAVE

LAKE 1

LAKE 2

LAKE 3

LAKE 4

WIGMORE HALL

BOULDER CHAMBER

CORBEL'S CHAMBER

STRAW CHAMBER (Ashwell Morgan's Palace)

LONG CRAWL

0

100

metres

Dan yr Ogof in 1937

38

THE SHOWCAVE

The development of the showcave commenced in 1938. A completely new entrance was established by blasting through the limestone cliffs, and concrete paths were laid inside the cave. Electric lighting was installed, powered by turbines driven by the water pouring from the cave itself. The showcave was opened to the public in August 1939 and proved a great attraction until it was forced to close at the onset of the Second World War. Even so, the site had its uses for the cave was quickly commandeered as a government store, and at one stage housed some 5,000 tons of TNT.

Peace returned in 1945 but the expected resumption of tourism failed to materialise. Due to family problems, the cave, for the next twenty years, was effectively 'out of bounds' to the public and cave explorers alike.

Nevertheless, a number of clandestine visits to Dan yr Ogof during this period revealed short

The tunnelling operations which lead to the opening of Dan yr Ogof showcave in 1939.

sections of new passageway. Apathy on the part of a growing number of sporting activists was not the reason for the lack of a concerted assault on the inner reaches of the cave, but rather a growing awareness of the tremendous possibilities at other sites in the Swansea valley. While cavers and potholers from the Mendip Hills, the Yorkshire Dales and Derbyshire had a good overall idea of the potential of limestone areas in England, it was only now that the

situation in Wales was becoming clearer. The picture was still hazy but the narrow band of limestone stretching from Pontypool, in the east, to Ammanford and beyond in the west seemingly contained a veritable treasure-trove of undiscovered caves. And nowhere was this potential greater than in the upper Swansea and Neath valleys.

It was the hillside opposite Dan yr Ogof which aroused the greatest interest in the period after the Second World War. Attention was focussed on the substantial spring known locally as Ffynnon Ddu (Black Spring), and it was the quest for the cave associated with the rising water that became the overriding concern of visiting cavers. Unlike the situation at Dan yr Ogof, where water poured out of the hillside via a large, spectacular tunnel, the water at Ffynnon Ddu welled quietly to the surface of a tranquil pool at the foot of a low cliff. The entrance to this cave was completely flooded. As early as 1942 the origin of the water rising from the dark tunnel had been identified. It lay two miles to the north-east, where a small mountain stream flowing south near the summit of Fan Gyhirych disappeared underground at the foot of a boggy and reedy recess known as Pwll Byfre.

At Easter 1946 a meeting of cavers was arranged at the Gwyn Arms, near Dan yr Ogof. Although the individuals concerned were deeply interested in Welsh caving, almost all were English, either members of, or associated with, organisations based in England. The main groups were the Welsh Branch of the Mendip Exploration Society, based in the Swansea valley; the Wessex Cave Club, based in the Ystradfellte area to the east; the University of Bristol Speleological Society; and the Dragon Group, whose members were drawn from various clubs and were led by Gerard Platten. The outcome of this gathering was the formation of the South Wales Caving Club. Later in the year a cottage, situated below Dan yr Ogof, was made available to the newly formed club, thanks to the generosity of Mr T. Ashwell Morgan. By 1947 the refurbished cottage was available for use and it became the base for many successful operations over the next twelve years. Today, the club owns a row of converted cottages, Powell Street, at Penwyllt. Indeed, the organisation has gone from strength to strength and is now probably the largest and most respected caving club in the country.

The meeting at Easter 1946 was, in fact, doubly significant. Among the group of explorers were a small number of specialists whose primary aim was to tackle the underwater tunnel at Ffynnon Ddu. These were the cave divers who, despite the very limited progress they were able to achieve in the Ffynnon Ddu spring, also took the opportunity to organise themselves formally. The Easter gathering was to result in the birth of the Cave Diving Group of Great Britain, the oldest diving club in the world.

Cavers felt certain that behind Ffynnon Ddu there must lie another vast stream stretching far to the east. The explorers did not have long to wait. On August Bank Holiday 1946

the cave was finally entered via a dry excavation close to the rising, which soon led to the discovery of a system over 5.5 km (3.5 miles) in length. The cave was named Ogof Ffynnon Ddu—Cave of the Black Spring. The complexity of this system gave even greater impetus to cave exploration, resulting in a series of projects which eventually culminated in the startling discoveries of the late 1960s.

In the context of Britain both Dan yr Ogof and Ogof Ffynnon Ddu were now firmly established as classic caves. From 1947 onwards until the early 1980s, Welsh caving became largely synonymous with the Swansea valley.

Discovered in 1946, the streamway in Ogof Ffynnon Ddu 1 is one of the finest in the British Isles.

The Long Crawl—Breakthrough and Triumph

Pwll Dwfn is Wales' deepest pothole. Its entrance is small and discreet and situated about half a mile from Dan yr Ogof.

Since 1946 cave exploration in the Swansea valley and adjoining areas has been dominated by the South Wales Caving Club. The establishment of the club heralded a golden age of exploration and discoveries came thick and fast. In 1947 the 93 m deep pothole, Pwll Dwfn, was found very close to Dan yr Ogof. Of even greater significance was the major extension to Tunnel Cave, discovered in December 1953. Here, a delicate excavation through a mass of large and precariously balanced boulders gave cavers access to a spectacularly large cavern and additional passageways that were to lead for upwards of 2 km. A new entrance was subsequently excavated high on the hillside which allowed cavers to make a complete traverse—in at one entrance and out at another—of the system. Later, in the mid 1970s, an altogether larger entrance was tunnelled into the complex, adjacent to the original point of entry. This facilitated the development of the extremely impressive Davy Price's Hall as a showcave. In view of the immensity of the cavern, to which the public have access, this lower section was renamed Cathedral Cave.

Pwll Dwfn: a caver on the second of the five shafts which must be descended to reach the bottom.

Entrance to Tunnel Cave high on the Black Mountain. Cavers can enter here, descend through the mountain and exit at Cathedral Cave several hours later.

Other finds were also being made. Across the valley to the east, not too far from the further reaches of Ogof Ffynnon Ddu, the 1 km long Pant Mawr Pot system was explored in the summer of 1953.

The discoveries at Dan yr Ogof were no less exciting. By studying the pattern of mapped passages it became clear that several kilometres of underground tunnels were still to be accounted for. However, despite the tremendous potential for discovery, activity at the cave was sporadic and often hampered by adverse weather. Numerous cavers attempted a variety of projects to try and access a 'back door' entrance. On the moorland high above Dan yr Ogof and several miles from the cave, were two prominent sites where water disappeared undergound: Sinc y Gïedd and Waun Fignen Felen. Both became the scene of determined efforts to excavate entries to passages which presumably lie below and connect with the main cave system at Dan yr Ogof. Stubbornly, both refused to capitulate, and still do.

Other changes also boosted cave exploration, not least the notable developments in caving equipment in the early 1960s: the appearance of rubber neoprene wetsuits to protect cavers from the icy cold (8°C) water, and the widespread use of electric lighting which led to the abandonment of the traditional carbide lamp, adopted by most cavers after the war. Alongside these technical developments, new or revitalised caving clubs began to appear, and fresh young faces. Swansea University Caving Club was particularly fortunate in the calibre of student which it attracted at this time and cavers such as Paddy O'Reilly, Susan Bradshaw (later O'Reilly), Colin Fairbairn and Pete Ogden became closely associated with various projects in the upper Swansea valley area.

The situation at Dan yr Ogof changed dramatically in 1964 when cavers were officially readmitted. South Wales Caving Club member Alan Coase was soon to take up the gauntlet. In November 1964, at the hitherto insignificant side passage between Lake 3 and 4, Alan, Frank Baguley and friends uncovered the Siphon Series. This very unpleasant—low, muddy and very wet—complex was to shed new light upon the route taken by the main river 'lost' in

A view of Davy Price's Hall, as it was originally named. This section of Tunnel Cave has been developed as a showcave and is now known as the Cathedral Cave.

Waun Fignen Felen, a substantial but rapidly eroding peatbog which drains into a stream sink. The water eventually finds its way to the River Llynfell which emerges at the entrance to Dan yr Ogof.

Cave diver Luke Devenish about to submerge in Tunnel Cave (Cathedral Cave) in the mid 1950s. The apparatus in use was oxygen 'rebreather' equipment, the forerunner of compressed air, open-circuit equipment which is the norm today.

Charles George, the leading Welsh diver of the 1960s, demonstrating the equipment used for cave diving prior to 1960.

the depths of Lake 4. The new discovery gave to cave divers an opportunity to advance but, despite the finding of Lake 5 and 6, the underwater terrain beyond proved problematic. Following a 10 m dive, the experienced explorer Charles George reached a substantial air chamber above the waters of Lake 7, but failed to penetrate the highly complex flooded section beyond. The underwater route leading into the mountain was seemingly unassailable.

At the limit of exploration in the 1937 Series there were: areas of complex geological faulting; sections of collapsed roof, or boulder chokes; several climbs, and an intricate network of crawlways. But of all these barriers the fabled Long Crawl was perhaps the most interesting and promising. It was a strategically sited passage with an enticing draught. A flow of air at any

blockage, climb or crawlway is a sure indicator of 'open' passage somewhere beyond. The determined caver will then do his or her utmost to follow the draughting tunnel in the hope that the situation will quickly improve. The Long Crawl, however, was particularly claustrophobic, a body-sized circular tube which twisted and meandered over a distance of about 100 m, supposedly coming to an 'end' at an extremely uncompromising squeeze. That the passage continued was evident; whether one could turn around or reverse along this tunnel was another matter. The doubt at the back of a caver's mind was obvious: if you committed yourself to squeezing forward, would you be able to get out again?

Having apparently ruled out easier options, Alan Coase enlisted his team to tackle the infamous Crawl. Fortuitously,

The Long Crawl had been entered in 1937 but it was not until 1966 that the final section of constricted passageway was finally negotiated.

Eileen Davies communicates with the surface via a telephone cable installed by cavers as an emergency measure in the event of an accident or flooding.

Photograph by A. Coase.

Eileen Davies, an attractive young lady from the nearby village of Crai had taken up the sport at about this time. Eileen had progressed through the normal caving channels but her interest was now focussed on exploration. Graced with a slender frame, her particular strength lay in her ability to negotiate the most 'impossible' constrictions. In conditions which might appear terrifyingly claustrophobic, or impossible to those of larger physique and stature, Eileen had the composure to remain steadfast and calm. Gaps of some 18 cm (seven inches) in height—less than the span of an outstretched adult hand and frequently less than double this in width—might sound ridiculous for a human body to negotiate, but these are obstacles frequently tackled by those such as Eileen committed to the cause of cave exploration. With cool, calm confidence and firm resolve numerous passages were extended, thanks to Eileen,

who became the only person to see the inside of a number of challenging holes. Sooner or later it was inevitable that the Crawl would be revisited and a scheduled 'push' was set up for the end of October 1965. In the event, the weather ruled out any such attempt and for many months the water level at the lakes was prohibitively high. Access to the 1937 Series was either risky or impossible.

Historical shot of cavers carrying a rubber dinghy between the third and fourth lakes. Eileen Davies is the person with the yellow top at the front of the boat; Bruce Foster stands at the rear.

It was on 20 March 1966 when the conditions were finally deemed suitable and Eileen Davies led the way into the Long Crawl. Alan Coase stopped at the last comfortable resting spot while Eileen wriggled on, occasionally shouting back to report her progress and to enquire just where the 'terminal' constriction was supposed to be. She eventually reached a point where the body-sized tube ended abruptly at a rather more spacious chimney or pot leading vertically down. She reversed the length of the Long Crawl quite easily; it was evident that Eileen had successfully negotiated the squeeze and both she and Alan were highly excited. But before they could return and see what lay beyond, bad weather again intervened.

It was Easter 1966 before any return was possible. Although water levels were high, it hadn't rained for 24 hours when on the morning of 12 April the party of five cavers decided to try their luck once more. Lake 2 and 3 were joined; less than 30 cm of airspace was available above the water level. Psychologically, the situation was intimidating; the slightest rise in water and they could be trapped. Alan Coase recalls the scene:

Bruce Foster had been the obvious choice to follow Eileen through, and they set off with 25 feet [7.5 m] of ladder while Neil Anderson, Colin Graham and myself set about maypoling [a technique using a single or extended scaffold bars to gain access to openings high above a cave floor] in Shower Aven at the start of the Crawl. We had just climbed this when back came a speechlessly excited Bruce. After about five minutes we had deciphered that 'it went'. There was a big chamber below but they could not reach it as they had not got enough ladder. We quickly provided more but,

mindful of the water situation, Neil and I achieved record time back to the Show Cave, received a favourable report, and just as rapidly returned to the waiting Colin. Deciding at the outset that it was to be 'smallest first', I took up the position of rear-end-Charlie. The others wriggled through quite easily but I found it one helluva thrutch, but eventually extruded through the squeeze and reached the top of the chimney just as the others were returning after a first quick look around.

Neil, in fact, was on the ladder telling me all about it, and I all but had to climb over him to get down and see for myself. At the bottom was indeed a spectacularly

Cloud Chamber in 1966, shortly after the dramatic breakthrough.

Cloud Chamber is a breathtaking site, a huge cavern with several small grottos for the visitor to admire.

large chamber which pointed on into the mountain. Within a short while this was to be named Gerard Platten Hall, in honour of the leader of the 1937 Dragon Group of explorers. The excitement was incredible, everybody talking at once.

'It wasn't just a chamber . . .'

'The straws!'

'No. The Straws.'

'I feel like kissing somebody!'

'Try Eileen.'

'I haven't shaved.'

The next few hours were to prove the dream of every caver. Easy walking passages led on deep beneath the Black Mountain, past pools of tranquil clear water, through caverns aptly named Monk Hall (after a prominent red stalagmite) and Cloud Chamber. Here, amid the huge expanse of the dark-walled cavern, their fading cap lamps glistened on a ceiling adorned with thousands of densely packed stalactites.

With the major lead temporarily blocked by the deep, cold and winding Green Canal they quietly retraced their steps back through the silent galleries towards the Long Crawl and exit. Here, as Alan Coase remembers, they encountered another wonder:

As we passed by the Crystal Pool [approximately 150 m from the Crawl] we noticed a shadow, or was it a passage? We entered Flabbergasm Chasm having passed it by at least three times. And what a passage! It really defies description even now, but then, without a footprint along its entire length, it was truly magnificent. Whilst most of us were more or less struck dumb, Rod [Stewart]

48

found tongue and to his only printable adjective the passage owes its name. The rhyming slang and the 'Chasm' arise from the twenty feet [6 m] drop into the Canyon which we nearly christened when mistaking it for a shadow on the floor, just beyond the ten foot [3 m] straw pillar that is a fitting final formation in that passage.

We eventually resurfaced at 3 a.m. to find Dr Price awaiting us in the restaurant. We bombarded him with details of our finds, to be rewarded by the offer of anything edible we could lay our hands on.

At the far end of Flabbergasm Chasm is a delicate straw pillar over 2 metres long.

The passage walls in Flabbergasm Chasm are almost symmetrical.

At the far end of the Canyon, the main route from the Long Crawl to Cloud Chamber, lies the Candlewax formation, a calcite pillar bearing a remarkable likeness to candlewax.

The Highway is a substantial tunnel which leads cavers to the Rising, the sump which marks the end of Dan yr Ogof 2.

One curious point had emerged from the day's caving. When Eileen got to the bottom of the chimney, at the head of the ladder pitch leading to Gerard Platten Hall, she found the initials P.O. inscribed in the mud. Several days were to elapse before the mystery was solved. It turned out that Peter Ogden of Swansea University Caving Club had slightly enlarged and successfully negotiated the squeeze the previous October. It was he who had been the first to triumph at the Long Crawl but, owing to the inclement weather, the great discovery had eluded him.

Two days later, Eileen, Bruce Foster, Neil Anderson and Rod Stewart led a large party into the extensions—named Dan yr Ogof 2—to follow up the exploration. With the aid of an inflatable boat, the Green Canal was crossed and within the space of a few metres another major passage was encountered trending directly across their path. To the left, led to the roof of a huge chamber – The Abyss – which was eventually to form part of a round trip, passing almost directly beneath Gerard Platten Hall, taking in *en route* other notable spots such as Bakerloo Straight and the Washing Machine. In the opposite

direction to the Abyss, the team found its way via another series of very impressive tunnels to the Rising. Here a crystal clear stream flowed from a flooded opening, or sump, situated at the foot of a high climb. For the time being this was the 'end'.

Further wonders were soon discovered: Dali's Delight, an amazingly weird area of three-dimensional rock sculptures in which the artist Salvador Dali would indeed have taken delight; and Mazeways, a series of pristine, clean-washed interconnecting tubes carved in jet black rock and partially floored with coarse, white sand. These two exciting finds added about a kilometre apiece to the ever lengthening cave system but the explorers had their sights on much bigger discoveries. From the survey data, the plotted cave map and all other information at their disposal, certain basic trends were soon revealed. The passage heading north from the Green Canal to the Rising was a major branch of the system which, it was believed, continued towards the huge surface sink at Waun Fignen Felen.

It was the passage trending towards Waun Fignen Felen that was to be the scene of the next major advance. In mid September 1966 Terry Moon and Alan Coase managed to scale the rock wall directly above the Rising Sump and, at a height of some 24 m, discovered a small tube emitting a very good draught. The significance of the draught was not lost on the two cavers and in minutes they had scurried along the narrow corridor and emerged into altogether more exciting terrain. Large holes appeared in the floor,

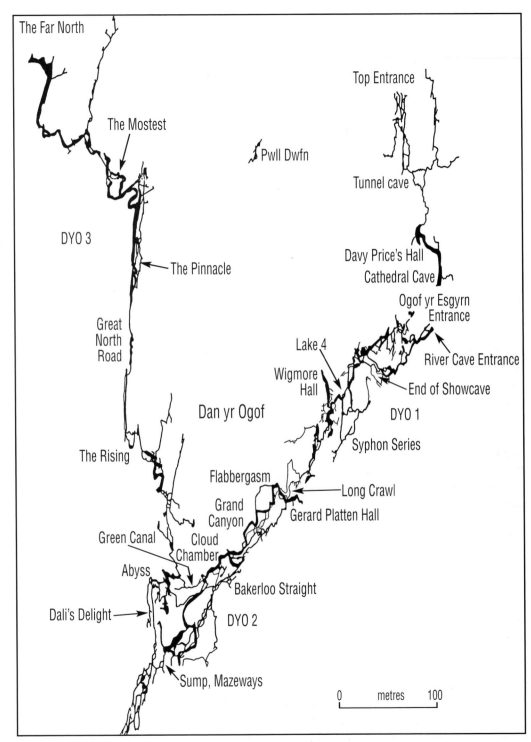

The Far North

The Mostest

Pwll Dwfn

Top Entrance

Tunnel cave

DYO 3

Davy Price's Hall

Cathedral Cave

The Pinnacle

Ogof yr Esgyrn
Entrance

Great
North
Road

Lake 4

River Cave Entrance

Wigmore
Hall

End of Showcave

Dan yr Ogof

DYO 1

Syphon Series

The Rising

Flabbergasm

Long Crawl

Grand
Canyon

Gerard Platten Hall

Green Canal

Cloud
Chamber

Abyss

Bakerloo Straight

Dali's Delight

DYO 2

Sump, Mazeways

0   metres   100

Dan yr Ogof in 1967.

51

disappearing into blackness. After crossing these obstacles they eventually reached a point where they could peer down a depth of 13-15 m and see the sandy bed of a stream—presumably the same stream which emerged from the sump at the Rising. A bypass to the obstacle had probably been found. Alan Coase recalls:

> Lack of time and tackle led us to turn back here, although those of us who could were back the next day. Terry had to go back to work, and the party was joined by Alan Murray and Susan Bradshaw. I descended first and quickly went down to the sump which was, as expected, only a short distance away. I returned to the ladder but, as there seemed to be a delay, I went on to the first corner to see if it continued. Indeed it did, high but narrow and in fact I had quite slowly rounded two more corners

before returning to the others. The atmosphere was as excited as on the first breakthrough, but the excitement had a subtle difference. On entering Flabbergasm Chasm, for example, we'd almost been silenced by the sheer beauty of the formations, the symmetry of the passage section and the scalloping. Now we were awed by sheer size rather than beauty. Entry to the Mostest, a fine meander containing excellent crystals, gours and flowstone, more than compensated, as did the fine sand formations near the end of the main passage.

The further they went, the larger became the passage until they reached the spectacular Pinnacle Chamber. Leaning away from the right wall of the chamber is a huge mass of rock which for all the world looks as though it could collapse into a pile

The Mostest lies at the very end of the Great North Road; here the wall is awash with fine flows of pure white calcite.

to as an aven when viewed from the bottom) near the Mostest, the party discovered a bypass around the blockage at the end of the Great North Road. Within a space of a few metres they were striding along the main northerly-trending tunnel towards a prominent junction which lay a short distance ahead. Beyond, the left-hand passage led them into the largest section of passage yet found in the system, the enormous Great Hall. Disappointingly, this ended in a massive jumble of boulders, a steep slope of debris extending from wall to wall and from floor to roof. This boulder choke has yet to be passed.

Two momentous advances had extended Dan yr Ogof to within a kilometre of Waun Fignen Felen. Here, however, the explorers encountered a major impasse. The cave had

The 13-m ladder pitch into the Great North Road is one of the more prominent obstacles *en route* to the further reaches of the cave. Rope and ladders must be transported the best part of 3 km to reach this point.

Pinnacle Chamber: like the Leaning Tower of Pisa, a huge section of cave wall has become detached at the northern end of the Great North Road.

of rubble at any time. Subsequent exploration of Dan yr Ogof 3, or the Great North Road as it became known, was to add little for several months, despite the successful penetration of the enormous boulder and sand choke, known as the Blackpool Sands. However, one day's advance, in September 1966, had added the best part of 1.5 km (a mile) to the cave's length which was aligned along the line of a massive fault in the Earth's crust.

In April 1967 David Judson and a small party from Yorkshire completed another dramatic advance. Following an exposed rock climb, up an ancient pothole (referred

The Great Hall lies at the terminus of the Far North, the furthest known extremity of Dan yr Ogof 3. Here the route forward is blocked by a massive area of roof collapse. It is presumed that the tunnel continues beyond the boulder choke.

been dramatically extended but it had not escaped the notice of the various activists that the Great North Road was, in fact, a side tunnel. The main river flowing through the system, that which plunged underground at Sinc y Gïedd on the moorland, about two miles south of Bannau Sir Gâr, had yet to be located. By pouring dye into the river at Sinc y Gïedd it was discovered that the water reappeared in the Mazeways area of the Lower Series in Dan yr Ogof 2, a fact which convinced Terry Moon, Colin Fairbairn and Richard Arculus to try and establish the course of the river through diving operations. A series of epic underwater ventures were to be undertaken at the end of Mazeways in 1968 and about 300 m

Sinc y Gïedd is a major stream sink, some 2 miles north-west of Dan yr Ogof.

of a branching passage was explored. But progress in this direction had seemingly reached its safe limit; motivation ebbed and the exploratory work ceased. Disappointingly, there was no indication of any additional dry passageways.

A major underground camp was organised for Easter 1968. Working from a base close to the Rising in Dan yr Ogof 2, many of the loose ends were tied up. The major part of the cave system was painstakingly surveyed to a high standard of accuracy and its length amounted to over 14 km (8.5 miles). The most exciting thing, however, was that the ultimate length of the cave was adjudged to be at least twice as long as its surveyed length. Where were the explorers to look next?

Adventures in the Deep—A Lucky Escape

1966 and 1967 were very important years in the history of Welsh caving. The discoveries at Dan yr Ogof had made headlines and attracted media attention in a big way. But the finds in Ogof Ffynnon Ddu, on the other side of the valley, were altogether more extensive and spectacular. In the summer of 1966 divers from the South Wales Caving Club and the Cave Diving Group finally broke free of the flooded passageways at the furthest point into the hillside. In the process they revealed the key to the entire system located behind the spring at Ffynnon Ddu. Wave after wave of discoveries revealed a labyrinth of passages several kilometres in length. In April 1967 a connection was finally established with Cwm Dŵr Quarry Cave, situated high upon the hillside at Penwyllt. Early in the summer of 1967 a third entrance—the Top Entrance—to the rapidly expanding system was revealed higher still on the mountainside.

Throughout 1967, therefore, exploration was being conducted at a frenzied pace on both sides of the Swansea valley. As if this were not exciting enough, the University of Bristol Spelaeological Society discovered yet another major system—the Little Neath River Cave—over in the next valley to the east. It is therefore hardly surprising that the Neath and Swansea valleys were to

Less than five minutes caving from the Top Entrance of Ogof Ffynnon Ddu lies the magnificent sight of the Mini Columns.

Little Neath River Cave: scaling a short waterfall.

Spectacular calcite formations in the Oxbow, Little Neath River Cave.

become the focus of the British speleological community at this time. Indeed, these cave systems were destined to become some of the finest in the world.

By 1970 the dust had began to settle. Ogof Ffynnon Ddu (OFD) was established as the longest and deepest cave in Britain with over 50 km of passageways and a vertical range of some 300 m. The system boasted wonderfully sculpted, clean-washed streamways, fabulous grottoes and classic through trips to tax and challenge all comers. OFD, as it is affectionately known in caving circles, has been extended to within a few hundred metres of the point where Nant Byfre disappears at the Pwll Byfre sink. On the eastern side of the Swansea valley, therefore, some of the main subterranean mysteries have largely been solved.

By contrast, the major part of the Dan yr Ogof system has still to be accounted for. The cave is unquestionably a classic in its own right with some of the finest caving that one could ever wish to undertake. A visit to the inner reaches of the cave, taking in the Lakes, the Long Crawl, Cloud Chamber, the Green Canal, the magnificent formations and the round trip, instils a very real sense of privilege couched in an atmosphere of deep mystery.

In 1970, there were many kilometres of cave awaiting discovery in Dan yr Ogof. The principal feeder, Sinc y Gïedd lies several miles to the north-west and it was conjectured that a vast network of passages was associated with this waterway, an illusive section of cave dubbed Dan yr Ogof 4, or the Gïedd Series. During the ensuing years this was the goal of many explorers but to gain access to this secret world, to breach the final frontier, would require bold measures. By this stage it was generally agreed that the key might well be revealed through diving, in a manner similar to that undertaken at Ogof Ffynnon Ddu.

Terry Moon, Richard Arculus and Colin Fairbairn had already made some bold forays into the dark and intimidating flooded tunnels of Dan yr Ogof in 1968. From conversations with these three it became clear that deep within the murky depths of Mazeways there were two principal branches heading in different directions. Neither had been fully explored. It was these leads which drew me to Dan yr Ogof in the summer of 1971.

The author, Martyn Farr, equipped with five lights, in the mid 1970s.

Beyond a lengthy dive, an explorer stands silhouetted in the fine sculpted tube directly above Lake 11 in Mazeways 2.

Mazeways was a particularly intriguing section of cave. As the name suggests, it was an area of spacious interconnecting tunnels carved in jet black rock, which in the space of several hundred metres led to a couple of static, brown and distinctly uninviting pools at the terminal point. Under normal conditions this complex area was free of any flowing water, yet everything about the place suggested that it could be radically different in time of flood. Dunes of coarse white sand marked the entry point to the series, and a cursory study of the walls and floor suggested that this was an enormous overflow passage. After heavy rain this series was evidently transformed to a raging underwater torrent!

It was August 1971 when I made my first attempt at the Mazeways sumps. I was to be joined by two other members of our club: my old schoolfriend Mike Wear and Bob Radcliffe. Enthusiastic support was forthcoming from other South Wales Caving Club members, and much of the heavy equipment was carried into the cave several days beforehand.

In less than one and a half hours travelling time from the entrance, we were sorting our various packages on a gravel beach. Prior to this operation I had never worn a spare set of diving apparatus (regarded as essential by cave divers today) and by the time I was fully kitted the additional encumbrance felt too unwieldy and clumsy to be of any practical benefit. This, I decided, was not the time or place to try and learn new techniques. I didn't want to risk any entanglement and by now I was perfectly happy with my normal breathing equipment, a demand valve which had served me well for more than a dozen dives.

Following the normal practice of underwater cave exploration, each diver, in turn, was to dive alone, aiming to follow the left-hand wall wherever it might lead. The water was heavily peat stained and very gloomy; it was like looking into a glass of cloudy beer. This would not be the most pleasant diving in the world but the conditions were as good as we were ever

A cave diver in the flooded tunnel at the end of Ogof Ffynnon Ddu 1. These conditions are typical of the flooded sections in Dan yr Ogof.

likely to experience. The passage was large and there was no doubt in anyone's mind that in flood it discharged a huge volume of water, probably from the missing section of the system.

The plan was simple. I would dive first and trail out a thin (4 mm diameter) line from a home-made spool or line reel. I would go as far as my nerve, or air supply, would permit. Upon my safe return, Mike and Bob would, in turn, try their hand. We discussed the communication signals which I would use on the line: two distinct pulls meant that I was coming back; three pulls meant I was through to an air pocket; more than three pulls spelt trouble! I then took a good deep breath, dipped under the surface and headed into the murk. A single lamp— my normal caving light—was adequate but made very little impression in the circumstances. It was just like being in a thick, dark fog; I could not see anything other than that within touching distance. Moving slowly forward, the passage began to slope away very gradually down to my right. Between my fins churning up the sediment on the floor and bubbles of my exhaled breath dislodging mud adhering to the cave roof, I could see little, if anything, to the rear. Thank goodness for the thin orange line, my only connection with safety.

My concentration was absolute. As I moved slowly forward through the tunnel I not only checked my guideline reel but also made sure that my ears were adjusting to the increased pressure. As usual, I stopped at a depth of about 2 m, squeezed my nose and went through the motions of 'equalising' the pressure. The eeeek-like sound from both ears confirmed that all was well, and that the pain generated by the increasing head of water above me was being kept at bay for the time being. Then it was on into the unknown. At 4-5 m depth I

Diving has been a valuable technique in cave exploration. Given its dangers there are very, very few practitioners of this most specialised of activities.

equalised again, and once more below that. I was feeling very tense but all was going well. By now the floor was free of sand and mud. The bare rock surfaces were well etched by water to form scallop markings, patterns which confirmed that I was heading upstream.

The line had been trailed out 25 m when suddenly and very much to my surprise I emerged into clear water. For all the world it was as though I had suddenly driven out of fog into a fine clear day. I stopped to take stock of my surroundings. The passage here was a substantial tube, about 4 m in diameter. I was kneeling on the smooth-washed floor: ahead the visibility was excellent, while to my right the seemingly undisturbed water hung like a dark veil.

I had now laid more line than on any of my previous exploratory dives. I looked at my pressure gauge; there was plenty of air left. Encouragingly, the tunnel was quite level for the next few metres and ahead of me I could dimly make out some form of enlargement. I moved on. A few metres further on there was a sloping ascent to my

left, while the right-hand wall disappeared into blackness in the opposite direction. I had evidently reached a junction.

Barely had I stopped to ponder the significance of the passage alignment than an altogether more traumatic discovery interrupted my train of thought. With all the drama of a lightning flash, my cool, tense composure was shattered: I had no air! I had just breathed out, but I could not breathe in! The unthinkable had happened. The valve had jammed. I was in no position to consider the manufacturer's stated 'fail safe' characteristics or the ironic 'lifetime guarantee' which it boasted. All I knew was that there was no burst of life-giving air flowing through the valve. Either I got out immediately or I was dead. My body was numbed: my brain traumatised. I grappled with the mouthpiece momentarily, then blind panic washed over me.

The deathly silence of the following minutes will never ever be erased from my mind. I had discarded the reel when the crisis hit and now I was finning with every last ounce of energy. It wasn't fast enough.

The craving for air was indescribable. I started to pull on the line in the forlorn hope that this might quicken my progress. Small silvery bubbles of air began to escape from the rubber exhaust valve on the faceplate of my mask. Like minute beads of mercury, one bubble after another ran up the glass and disappeared. It was as though life itself was escaping. I had no conception of distance, no thoughts of anything other than the next breath. Panic was master of all.

The next thing I remember was being forcibly halted. The line which I had laid on the way in now led me into a narrow crack in the wall. The horizontal undercut was quite impossible to pass. Had I been thinking at all rationally I would have been able to piece the information together and realise that, on the inward journey, the passage must have meandered away from a straight-line course; that the larger, passable tunnel lay somewhere off to my right. But I was no longer capable of thinking clearly and rationally.

I was gripped by an elemental craving for breath; for air, for anything to fill my empty lungs. Everything I had learned was forgotten in the utter desperation of the situation. I pulled out my mouthpiece and breathed water. It is strange to relate, even now, that somehow in the space of, perhaps, 30 or 45 seconds the will to survive was replaced by resignation to death. I was convinced that I was about to die.

Back at the surface, trouble was suspected. Bob voiced his concern:

'I think you'd better go in, Mike.'

In a matter of seconds Mike had made his final checks and waded out across the pool. He was a diver in the Royal Navy and had been trained to deal with such eventualities. But we had never before dived together in a cave and Mike had no way of knowing how I might react in any given emergency. He disappeared under the water wondering what on earth he was going to find. There was no longer any movement on the line. A minute or so later Mike resurfaced and announced,

'He's coming up.'

Mike had seen me in the undercut and blinded, perhaps, by my light shining towards him had assumed that I was heading out. However, I did not see him. Half a minute elapsed. My non-appearance prompted Mike to dive again. This time I saw him, or rather a bright halo-like effect which served to silhouette or frame Mike in the passage. After having lain on the floor in that narrow crack for some two minutes, the life-force within me was somehow rekindled. I drifted out and 'swam' under my own steam to the surface.

After a 28 m dive, which had taken me to a depth of 8 m, I was still alive—just. I gradually came around and after five minutes or so related the tale to my companions. I should have been dead; that I survived was miraculous. In all probability I had 'breathed' fresh water for over two minutes.

Mike made another short dive to retrieve the reel, then we carried all the gear out of the cave. This brush with death had such an effect upon the sensibilities of my comrades that neither Mike nor Bob ever made an exploratory cave dive again.

A caver negotiating a diving cylinder through the Long Crawl.

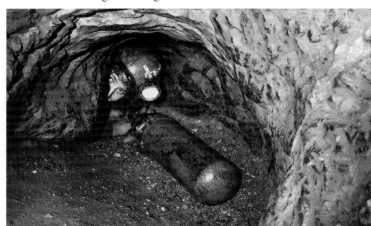

I, too, had learned the most important lesson of my life. I was so utterly and totally embarrassed by what had transpired. I was brought back to life and reality with an earth-shattering bump! Over the next few days I analysed and reanalysed the situation. But far from acting as a deterrent, the failure hardened my resolve; from now on I would guard against every eventuality.

In the weeks to follow I slowly rebuilt my confidence. From now on I would be proficient in the use of a reserve system. Soon the 'What if?' questions were answered. I now had a better idea about my own limitations. While on the one hand the prospect of tackling Mazeways again was extremely daunting, the lure of those missing miles in Dan yr Ogof was like some addictive drug.

It was December before I retraced my dive in the Mazeways sump. Passing beyond the scene of the near catastrophe was psychologically difficult but once I re-emerged, unscathed, at dive base it was as though the ghosts of the recent past had been laid to rest. In January, I ventured further and tied the line off some 92 m from base. The most exciting thing was that at 80 m I noticed a few centimetres of silvery surface, and had the water level in the cave been lower I would have been able to stand head and shoulders above the water in an airbell, a breathable pocket of air. Apart from providing welcome relief, it would also serve as an advance dive base for the flooded section ahead.

The summer of 1972 was to witness another significant development, for it was then I teamed up with Roger Solari, a Royal Forest of Dean Caving Club member. In superb weather conditions the challenge at Dan yr Ogof now assumed a greater priority than any other project, and in mid July Roger assisted me by carrying in some of the equipment. On arrival, the water levels were very low and, as suspected, there was now a substantial airbell at 80 m. Here I was able to stop, rest, breathe normal cave air and prepare myself psychologically for the next stage.

After a couple of minutes, I pressed on and began laying fresh line into the unknown. One false turning took me up a dead-end side tunnel, but after retracing my steps for a short distance the main route forward was quickly found. A small rock step led into a low, wide tunnel rather less than half a metre (18 inches) in height at its most restricted point. Knowing full well what could happen should a passage such as this meander, I took the precaution of wrapping the line around large stones at frequent intervals. In such a way I was reassured that, on exit, when visibility might be no more than a few centimetres, I could follow the tried and tested route. I didn't intend getting jammed in an undercut ever again! Gradually the passage became larger and slightly deeper. I tied off the line to a rock at 108 m from dive base and came out feeling very pleased.

The following week was perfect for another attempt. On this occasion Roger was to dive first and explore as far as his single bottle would permit. This contained approximately 26 minutes worth of air at the depth in which we were operating. But, given our air safety margins, it meant that Roger would be able to dive into the tunnel for a maximum of eight minutes, for safety rules dictated that after one third of his air had been used he had to start upon his exit. In theory, therefore, he would arrive back on the surface, at dive base, with eight minutes worth of air still in the bottle—an emergency supply for any unforeseen difficulty which might arise on the way out. After Roger had completed his dive, I planned to continue the exploration using a bottle that was almost twice the size that he was using. In theory, therefore, and barring any mishaps, I should have been able to proceed a good way further than Roger.

Three of us went into the cave that day: Roger, Mike Coburn and I. The carry in was physically hard and having set Roger on his way we were glad of a rest. Twenty minutes went by and Mike raised his eyebrows. After thirty minutes we were both very concerned. He only had 26 minutes of air. Even if he had overcome a problem and had made it to the safety of the airbell, I knew that he would not want to spend much time there. I left Mike with the parting shot,

'If I'm not back in an hour we're on to something.'

I slid cautiously into the water and Mike went for a wander to try and get himself warm.

The thin orange line led me on past the previous week's limit. A dip, a wall of boulders on the right, a larger section 3 m in diameter, but still there was no sign of Roger.

'He's doing well,' I thought.

Nevertheless, my stomach was churning with anxiety and that nagging question was only just kept at bay: suppose something had happened to him? Suddenly, the line turned upwards; at 118 m from base the roof disappeared and I went straight up into an airspace.

There in front of me, carefully placed on a narrow ledge was a single set of diving equipment. Great, Roger was safe! Above the ledge, a small crawl-cum-stooping passage led off into the blackness. I turned my air supply off and stowed my gear carefully to one side. The fact that there was no sign of Roger had to be a good omen. My imagination was running riot—huge caverns beyond our wildest dreams! Just what had he discovered?

I pounded along the passage, my thoughts racing with a mixture of envy and excitement. Suddenly, 60 m from where I'd left my kit I located the missing explorer. Roger was groping his way along a dismal canal passage, three quarters full of water. In his hand he was clutching our line reel and in the process of winding the cord back on the drum.

'Well done, Roger,' I exclaimed before a few other expletives fell from my lips.

'It wouldn't be so bad if I could actually see what's here,' he replied. 'You haven't brought my glasses, have you?'

'Sorry?'

Having left his specs with Mike, Roger was all but blind and was relying solely on the line to lead him back to his kit!

'We're on to something here all right,' he said. 'I reckon I've covered 120 to 180 metres and there seem to be holes all over the place.'

It was so funny. Roger had made the biggest discovery in the cave for a couple of years, quite possibly Dan yr Ogof 4 itself, but he couldn't describe what he had found!

About 245 m of 'dry' passages were quickly explored and another four sumps located. The most promising lead was a very large, high-level passage set tantalisingly above an impossible 4 m climb. Being able to peer up and speculate was downright frustrating for we were both reasonable climbers, but without a rope or any other climbing aid there was absolutely nothing we could do. Amid the excitement we were totally oblivious of the time and since neither of us possessed a diving watch, there was no way of knowing how long we had been away. When we finally made our way out Mike was greatly relieved; he'd been on his own for over four hours. He was so cold it was all he could do to raise a smile.

'This'll cost you a pint, Farr.'

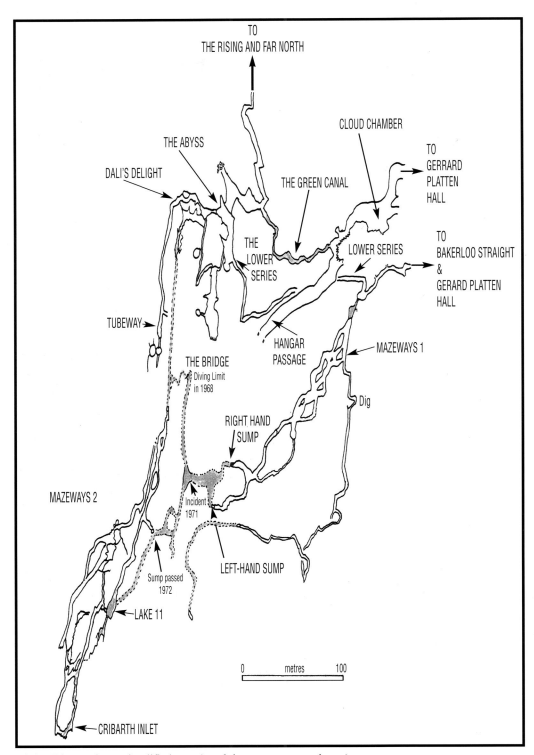

TO
THE RISING AND FAR NORTH

CLOUD CHAMBER

THE ABYSS

TO
GERRARD
PLATTEN
HALL

DALI'S DELIGHT

THE GREEN CANAL

THE
LOWER
SERIES

LOWER SERIES

TO
BAKERLOO STRAIGHT
&
GERRARD PLATTEN
HALL

TUBEWAY

HANGAR
PASSAGE

MAZEWAYS 1

THE BRIDGE
Diving Limit
in 1968

Dig

RIGHT HAND
SUMP

MAZEWAYS 2

Incident
1971

LEFT-HAND SUMP

Sump passed
1972

LAKE 11

0   metres   100

CRIBARTH INLET

Diving Discoveries: a simplified map (overlying passages not shown).

Two weeks later we were back, equipped with boots and everything we needed to reach the high-level opening. The climb was something akin to trying to reach a body-sized hole set in the middle of a high ceiling. Without anything to stand on, it was hopeless. In the event a much simpler solution presented itself. Fashioning a rope into a coil we lassooed a knobbly rock projection and in no time at all I heaved myself up. The rope was then made properly secure and Roger joined me. A superb, clean-washed, circular tubeway within which water evidently flowed during flood conditions, lay ahead of us. Beaming with smiles we almost broke into a run. Passing a junction, the main route veered to the left. Within seconds of entering this section of passage a tremendous roar of water could be heard away in the distance.

'Can you hear that?' asked Roger.

'Bloody hell!'

We were now caving at a frenzied pace. It had to be the long lost main stream. I was leading at this point but Roger was close on my heels.

'Blast, it's choked solid,' I screamed in disappointment.

'It can't be.'

'It is, I tell you.'

We split up. Surely some opening or other hereabouts would gain us access to the passages beyond. Roger started looking up at the roof; I set to on pulling out rocks at floor level. Judging by the sound, the blockage could only be a metre or so wide, and there wasn't much holding the boulders in place. Rubble and stones were hurled aside in a demonic fury. This was exploration fever at its height. In fifteen minutes or so I was through.

'I'm there! Come on! Hurry up!'

Roger appeared as though from nowhere. We scrambled through a three-dimensional maze of passageways and reached our goal.

Our faces fell. We could not believe it! One glance at the size of the stream was enough to convince us that this was not the long sought after main river; it was a large feeder stream, not all that much smaller than the stream from the Far North in Dan yr Ogof 3. The beckoning roar which we had heard minutes previously was generated by water cascading over a 1.3 m waterfall. How deceptive . . . and so disappointing.

But we soon overcame our disappointment for there were inviting passages leading off all over the place. Each was checked out in turn and the tally of new passage began to climb. We spent six hours in the new extension that day before fatigue began to set in. The discoveries were not in the form of immense caverns, or indeed the exquisite beauty and fragility of formations encountered on previous breakthroughs, but the Divers' Extensions or Mazeways 2 were a very significant discovery and added 1.5 km (a mile), with a further 400 m underwater, to the length of the cave system, now in excess of 15 km. While the sighting of some water from Sinc y Gïedd had been exciting, it was acutely frustrating not to be able to follow it for any distance. Above the waters of the underground stream a series of massive roof falls seemed totally impregnable.

In the weeks and months that followed we persevered with all the enthusiasm we could muster, until finally work ceased.

As is so often the case, for the next five years the exploration in this sector of the system underwent a period of quiescence. Other projects, other caves, assumed a greater priority. In 1974 Roger Solari lost his life in a tragic cave-diving accident elsewhere in South Wales and for a while underwater activity was set back. Then, in 1978, there was a renewed burst of enthusiasm. Digging above water at the

Lake Chamber in Mazeways 3 is one of the more remote sections of the system, a sector of the cave which may eventually lead to another major breakthrough.

An elaborate syphoning project – to drain a blocked underwater tunnel – was undertaken in Mazeways 3 in the early 1980s. To date this tunnel still thwarts all attempts to pass.

southern terminus of Mazeways 2 our small team discovered another 440 m. Once again, complex passage development was observed on several different levels and the new find was to be named Mazeways 3.

That there is tremendous potential in this south-westerly sector of the system cannot be doubted, but since 1978 no significant headway has been made; every route forward appears to be hopelessly blocked with boulders. The situation is one of complete stalemate. The Mazeways area is the furthest known point in Dan yr Ogof where the water from Sinc y Gïedd can be seen and, as such, it is a strategic part of the cave. Excavation may be possible although tremendous commitment would be required. One thing is assured: the water has and always will find a way through. For this reason there seems little doubt that a route back through the mountain does exist. What will surely drive the true explorer onward is the quest for the key.

The Lure of the Unknown

Enthusiasm, dedication and determination are crucial elements in any success story. Each new generation of aspiring cave explorers must build upon the foundations laid by their predecessors. Today this means that much research must be undertaken before a project gets underway: reports must be analysed, manpower considerations need to be assessed, and weather conditions studied. Some projects may be undertaken in the space of a single day, whilst others may entail a rolling programme involving the establishment of underground camps when the right set of circumstances arise.

The underworld is never short of surprises. Caves which have been known for many years can occasionally yield their secrets. That thorough research and dedication pays off was clearly demonstrated by a series of discoveries in 1990 and 1991. The finds by Nick Geh, Pat Cronin, the late Brian Murlis and friends demonstrated that nothing should be taken at face value. Over 900 m of new passage was discovered by this team in Dan yr Ogof 1, some 750 m of which was found beyond a short, 15 m long sump at the head of the River Cave, just a few minutes from the cave entrance! This series was named the Battle of Britain Series to commemorate the 50th anniversary of the aerial assault on the major cities of Britain during the Second World War.

At the same time that renewed interest had arisen in the digging and diving sphere, Liam Kealy and another team began a long-term assault on some of the unclimbed openings high above the floor in Dan yr Ogof 3. Given the geological characteristics of this sector of the mountain, in particular the complex faulting, it is reasonable to anticipate the existence of a set of parallel passageways heading in a northerly direction. Operating out of an isolated base camp in

Gwyn Saunders Hall, a huge cavern, lies a few metres from the Dan yr Ogof showcave, unknown and unexplored until its discovery by divers in 1991.

At the western end of the Black Mountain, caves such as Ogof Pasg, near Brynaman, give an indication of the many caves waiting to be discovered.

the Far North, a series of mini expeditions were rewarded for their perseverance. Some 500 m of new passageway was discovered – the High and Mighty Series – but, disappointingly, the group could find no way of bypassing the huge boulder collapse at the northern extremity of the cave.

This delicate crystal pool in Wellington Passage, Battle of Britain Series, illustrates the fragility of the cave environment.

Much research is currently underway to locate new caves. Highly sophisticated equipment, such as resistivity apparatus or ground radar, may be adopted on occasions in an effort to detect underground passages. Clive Jones has been a pioneer of this hi-tech approach in Wales.

Apart from exploratory work conducted within the cave, other activities have taken place on the surface and in the numerous shallow caves, or 'digs', believed to be associated with the Dan yr Ogof system. There are a number of streams, large and small, which disappear on the southern slopes of the Black Mountain, and many have been dye-traced to Afon Llynfell emerging at Dan yr Ogof. Over the years all of these potential cave sites have been assessed and some have witnessed periods of intense activity in an attempt to try and gain access to the passageways which exist below. The major stream sink at Waun Fignen Felen, for example, lies less than a mile and a half north-west of the entrance to Dan yr Ogof and may well prove to be a possible 'back door' to the cave system.

The Cribarth Sink, about half a mile south-west of Craig-y-Nos, is one of many places where small surface streams disappear underground. The cave beneath was entered for the first time in 1998 and has been explored for several hundred metres.

The water which disappears here has been traced to Dan yr Ogof 3. Approximately 1 km separates Waun Fignen Felen from the massive roof fall which terminates the cave in the Far North. On several occasions large teams have tackled the boulder blockage which obstructs entry at the sink, and in the late 1960s a shaft was sunk to a depth of 30 m. However, no open cave passage has been encountered to date.

Digging in the muddy confines of Cribarth Sink Cave.

The most intriguing site of all is Sinc y Gïedd, situated some 2 miles north-west of Dan yr Ogof. No matter how large the floods pouring off Bannau Sir Gâr to the north, this short section of cave seems perfectly capable of swallowing the entire river. Not surprisingly, therefore, this cave has always been the prime contender for a 'back door' to Dan yr Ogof. Regretably, vast quantities of silt and gravel have been swept into the cave in recent years and as a consequence passages which were negotiable in the mid 1940s and in 1970 are no longer accessible. Whether nature itself will solve the problem or whether it may prove possible to re-excavate these passages remains to be seen.

To the north and west of Afon Gïedd lie several other places where surface streams disappear tantalisingly into the ground. To the west of and closest to Sinc y Gïedd is a site known as Ogof Carreg Lem, a system over 300 m in length, first explored in 1981. Collapsed boulders subsequently blocked the entrance but the cave was reopened in 1997 to facilitate renewed exploration in its further reaches. North of Ogof Carreg Lem is another sink known as the Rusty Horseshoe Dig, and yet further north there is a promising shallow hole at Twyn Tal y Ddraenen. Here, in the early 1990s, Tony Baker, Martin Hoff and friends discovered over 200 m of passageways with a vertical range of 23 m. Any one of these sites could so easily provide the long sought after key to the missing miles of Dan yr Ogof, for dye introduced at these points finds it way to Dan yr Ogof in the space of 48 hours. In all probability, therefore, the passageways beneath the

Considerable commitment and effort was required to access Cribarth Sink, and equal determination will be required to extend the cave further. Tony Donovan before and after an exploratory trip.

Black Mountain will be, in the fullness of time, one of the most extensive cave systems in the British Isles. Dan yr Ogof is destined to become one of the longest caves in the country. It is not unreasonable to speculate that the cave, currently 16 km long, will be 40 km or more within the next 10 years.

Geological and hydrological studies suggest that the greatest potential for further discoveries lies beneath that area of mountain adjacent to Cribarth. This is where the water from Sinc y Gïedd, Ogof Carreg Lem, Rusty Horseshoe and Ogof Twyn Tal y Ddraenen reappears. The challenge posed by this south-westerly sector of the system is great, but the cave is nothing if not fickle. So often a cave explorer can toil away for months or even years at a blockage to no avail. But then, out of the blue, a lucky break will be made and exploration will surge forward at breathtaking speed.

Dan yr Ogof has always been synonymous with mystery and challenge. Indeed, the challenges posed by Dan yr Ogof today are every bit as great as when the Morgan brothers of Abercrave embarked upon their audacious quest in 1912. Our knowledge of geography, geology,

hydrology and other facets of cave science has vastly improved during the past 90 years, yet despite all the information at our disposal we are still unsure as to how many caves remain to be discovered in the Swansea valley. Man may have been to the Moon and conducted studies in outer space but we have much still to learn about the wonders beneath our feet.

The upper Swansea valley is a particularly wild and beautiful area of the British Isles. For tranquility and sheer solitude Bannau Sir Gâr and the Black Mountain are unsurpassed. To venture across the boulder strewn moorland above and beyond Dan yr Ogof is to commune

A caver negotiates the rope ascent to the Top Entrance of Tunnel Cave.

with nature. At places like Waun Fignen Felen and Sinc y Gïedd there is little—with the exception of sheep—to remind the walker of the imprint of human civilisation. For those in search of wild Wales this place, now the occasional haunt of the rare and majestic red kite, is heaven. Yet deep underground, removed still further from civilisation, lies the serene underground world, one of the last true wilderness areas of the planet.

Dan yr Ogof is indeed a portal to a dark and timeless world. A journey into the depths of the Black Mountain is to experience true wonder and a rare sense of privilege. Dan yr Ogof epitomises the very best of British caving; it is the jewel in the crown of Wales' underworld.

A Glossary of Caving Terms

Abseil: A method of descending vertical rock utilising a hand-held friction device on a rope.

Active cave: A cave with a flowing stream.

Bed: A layer or stratum in a sequence of sedimentary rock.

Bedding plane: A plane of separation between two layers of rock. Prominent bedding planes often produce wide, low-roofed passages.

Bivouac: A temporary camp established on a long-distance cave expedition.

Boulder choke: A pile of rocks or boulders, as from a collapsed roof, blocking a passage.

Calcite: Calcium carbonate in crystalline form, the main constituent of limestone.

Carbide lamp: A lamp lit by burning acetylene gas, produced by the action of water on calcium carbide.

Chimney: A narrow, vertical or steeply-inclined fissure.

Chockstone: A rock wedged in a crack; can be used for assistance, as in climbing, or as a physical support, e.g. in a boulder choke.

Column: A pillar-like formation linking cave roof and floor, usually formed by the joining of a stalactite and stalagmite.

Crawl: A low passage through which progress can only be made on hands and knees, or flat-out.

Curtain: A thin, fluted sheet or draping of dripstone; sometimes a row or group of regularly-shaped stalactites.

Dig: An excavation above or below ground to find a new cave or section of passage.

Dip: The inclination of a bed of rock, its angle from the horizontal being expressed in degrees. It is measured by a clinometer.

Doline: Surface hollow caused by solution or collapse of an underground cave.

Duck: A point where the roof slopes to meet the water level, or where there is little airspace, traversed by a quick duck or dive.

Flowstone: A continuous sheet of calcite, covering a cave wall or floor.

Fluorescein: A harmless green dye, used for tracing underground water and its point of emergence.

Formation: Any decorative cave deposit, including stalactites, stalagmites and helictites.

Gour: A rimstone pool formed by deposits of calcite.

Helictite: A small stalactite displaying erratic or eccentric growth.

Joint: A division or crack, often vertical, through a bed of rock.

Karabiner: A metal snap-link used for fastening ropes to anchor points, connecting ladders etc.

Lifeline: A safety rope, to protect a caver on vertical sections underground.

Lycopodium: Spores produced by the lycopodium fern may be dyed and used in water tracing experiments.

Phreatic cave: A cave formed below the water-table.

Pitch: A vertical section of cave, usually requiring the use of a ladder or rope.

Pothole: A vertical shaft, either open to the sky or inside a cave.

Resurgence: The point at which underground water emerges at the surface, as in a spring.

Rimstone pool: A small basin with a calcareous edge deposited by thin films of calcite-bearing water.

Rising: A point where underground water rises to the surface.

Shaft: A vertical entrance to a mine or pothole.

Sinkhole: A place where water sinks or previously disappeared underground.

Siphon: A place in a cave passage which is normally totally flooded.

Speleology: The exploration and scientific study of caves.

Squeeze: A narrow place just large enough for a human body to wriggle through.

Stalactite: A formation, usually of calcite, hanging from a cave roof.

Stalagmite: A formation growing upwards from a cave floor.

Strike: An imaginary horizontal line along a bedding plane, at right angles to the true dip.

Sump: A point often at the far end of a cave where water prevents further exploration. Short sumps can be negotiated by holding one's breath; longer sumps require the use of specialist equipment.

Swallet: An opening in limestone where a stream flows underground.

Swallow hole: An opening through which a stream disappears and flows underground.

Water-table: The upper surface of waterlogged unconsolidated deposits or rock. The phreatic zone lies below the water-table.

Appendix
Cave Access and Conservation

Caves are a very special field of sporting and recreational potential. They are also a unique and vulnerable part of our national and cultural heritage. Today Dan yr Ogof and several other caves of the upper Swansea valley are internationally acclaimed for their beauty and scientific importance. They contain evidence of landscape and cultural history as well as climatic change. They are, therefore, places to be treated with respect, sites which require careful attention if they are to be conserved for the benefit and enjoyment of future generations.

Cavers and all who venture underground must accept responsibility for cave conservation. Put simply, this means that we should all try and leave a cave in a better state than we found it. We can all undertake small tasks, such as removing a sweet wrapper which has been accidentally dropped, or re-adjust a length of conservation tape. But site conservation also requires a close working relationship between landowners, cavers and the various statutory conservation agencies. It is through such partnerships that any potential threats to the cave environment—present or future—can be removed or minimised.

Cave access and environmental conservation are becoming increasingly complex matters. All land is owned by someone and those participating in outdoor recreation must take note of this fact and act accordingly. By respecting the rights of landowners and following the Country Code, access will hopefully be ensured for future generations.

Those people who may wish to further their interest in caves are strongly recommended to seek professional advice, undertake appropriate training at a specialist centre, and join a caving club. Cave guidebooks have been published for all the caving regions of the British Isles, but whilst these are extremely useful there is no substitute for the information, knowledge and experience which the novice will acquire by joining a club.

Many caves in South Wales are accessible to enthusiasts at virtually any time. However, in the case of larger cave systems a number of different organisations may be involved in cave related matters. For example, there is no right of entry at Dan yr Ogof or Cathedral Cave, as both sites are part of a private showcave complex. The entrances to Ogof Ffynnon Ddu are also gated and locked. Other bodies with an important conservation and administrative role with regard to the management of the sites and their environs include the Brecon Beacons National Park Authority, the Countryside Council for Wales, and the Dan yr Ogof Advisory Committee.

Access arrangements to Dan yr Ogof have been formalised. Entry is permitted under a leader scheme implemented by the Dan yr Ogof Advisory Committee. All parties wishing to visit the cave must be accompanied by a recognised leader, who has a clear responsibility as a Cave Conservation Warden. Group size is limited to five and special projects, such as digging and scientific study, require the approval of the Advisory Committee. Novices are not allowed beyond the Long Crawl.

Much of the Black Mountain has been designated a SSSI—Site of Special Scientific Interest (the Mynydd Du SSSI was designated in 1963 and extended in subsequent years)—and a management plan has been prepared for all the caves in the area. The future well-being of this precious and fragile environment lies in our hands; let us do our utmost to protect the area for the benefit of those who will follow.

The Secretary
South Wales Caving Club
1-10 Powell Street
Penwyllt
Near Abercrave
SA9 1GQ

General Information:
Dan yr Ogof Showcaves
Abercrave
Glyntawe
SA9 1GJ
Tel: 01639 730284/730693